A-LEVEL YEAR 2

STUDENT GUIDE

OCR

Chemistry A

Module 5

Physical chemistry and transition elements

Mike Smith

PHILIP ALLAN FOR

HODDER EDUCATION

AN HACHETTE UK COMPANY

Philip Allan, an imprint of Hodder Education, an Hachette UK company, Blenheim Court, George Street, Banbury, Oxfordshire OX16 5BH

Orders

Bookpoint Ltd, 130 Park Drive, Milton Park, Abingdon, Oxfordshire OX14 4SE

tel: 01235 827827

fax: 01235 400401

e-mail: education@bookpoint.co.uk

Lines are open 9.00 a.m.–5.00 p.m., Monday to Saturday, with a 24-hour message answering service. You can also order through the Hodder Education website: www.hoddereducation.co.uk

© Mike Smith 2016

ISBN 978-1-4718-5928-1

First printed 2016

Impression number 5 4 3 2 1

Year 2020 2019 2018 2017 2016

This guide has been written specifically to support students preparing for the OCR A-level Chemistry A examinations. The content has been neither approved nor endorsed by OCR and remains the sole responsibility of the author.

Typeset by Integra Software Services Pvt. Ltd, Pondicherry, India

Printed in Italy

Hachette UK's policy is to use papers that are natural, renewable and recyclable products and made from wood grown in sustainable forests. The logging and manufacturing processes are expected to conform to the environmental regulations of the country of origin.

Contents

■ Getting the most from this book

Exam-style questions

Commentary on the questions

Tips on what you need to do to gain full marks, indicated by the icon **e**

Sample student answers

Practise the questions, then look at the student answers that follow.

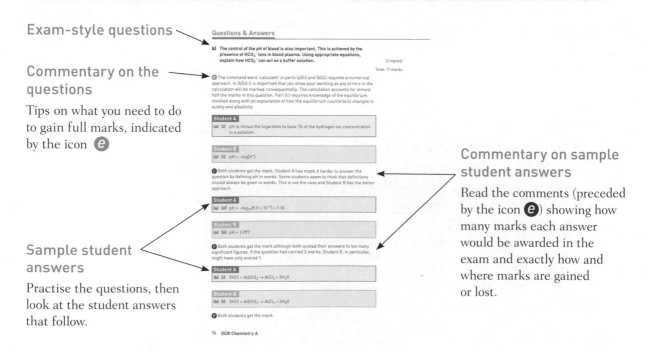

Commentary on sample student answers

Read the comments (preceded by the icon **e**) showing how many marks each answer would be awarded in the exam and exactly how and where marks are gained or lost.

◼ About this book

This guide is the third of a series covering the OCR Chemistry A specification for A-level. It offers advice for the effective study of Module 5: Physical chemistry and transition elements. This module, together with Modules 1 and 2 (covered in the first student guide in this series) and Module 3 (covered in the second student guide in this series) is examined in the A-level Component 1 exam and as part of the synoptic Component 3 exam, which draws on all the modules, from 1 to 6.

The **Content Guidance** gives a point-by-point description of all the facts you need to know and concepts that you need to understand for Module 5. It aims to provide you with a basis for your revision but you will also need to use other sources.

The **Questions & Answers** section shows you the sorts of questions you can expect in the component test. It would be impossible to give examples of every kind of question in one book, but the questions used should give you a flavour of what to expect. Each question has been attempted by two students, Student A and Student B. Their answers, along with the comments, should help you to see what you need to do to score marks — and how you can easily *not* score marks even though you probably understand the chemistry.

What can I assume about the guide?

You can assume that:

- the topics covered in the Content Guidance relate directly to those in the specification
- the basic facts and major concepts are stated clearly and explained
- the questions at the end of the guide are similar in style to those that will appear on the exam paper
- the answers supplied are genuine, combining responses commonly written by students
- the standard of the marking is broadly equivalent to the standard that will be applied to your answers

What can I *not* assume about the guide?

You must *not* assume that:

- every last detail has been covered
- the way in which the concepts are explained is the only way in which they can be presented in an exam (concepts are often presented in an unfamiliar situation)
- the range of question types presented is exhaustive (examiners are always thinking of new ways to test a topic)

Study skills and revision techniques

All students need to develop good study skills and this section provides advice and guidance on how to study A-level chemistry.

It is a good idea to check your notes using textbooks and to fill in any gaps. Make sure that you go back and ask the teacher if you are unsure about anything, especially if you find conflicting information in your class notes and textbook.

It is essential to file your notes in specification order, using a consistent series of headings. The Content Guidance section can help you with this.

Preparation for exams is a personal thing. Different people prepare, equally successfully, in different ways. The key is being honest about what works *for you*.

The scheme outlined below is a suggestion as to how you might revise for Module 5 over 3 weeks. The work pattern is fairly simple but you must adapt it to suit your style of revising.

Day	Week 1	Week 2	Week 3
Mon	Rates of reaction: 20 min	Rates of reaction. Write summary notes and attempt questions from books or papers: 30 min	The exam paper: 100 marks in 135 min Try a past paper 1, spread over two nights. List anything that you are unsure of and ask your teacher for help
Tues	K_c, K_p, pH and buffers: 20 min Rates of reaction: 10 min	K_c, K_p, pH and buffers Write summary notes and attempt questions from books/papers: 30 min	
Wed	Lattice enthalpy, ΔH and ΔS: 20 min K_c, K_p, pH and buffers: 10 min Rates of reaction: 5 min	Lattice energy, ΔH and ΔS Write summary notes and attempt questions from books or papers: 30 min	Try a second past paper spread over two nights. List anything that you are unsure of and ask your teacher for help
Thurs	Electrode potentials and fuel cells: 20 min Lattice energy, ΔH and ΔS: 10 min K_c, K_p, pH and buffers: 5 min Rates of reaction: 1 min	Electrode potentials and fuel cells. Write summary notes and attempt questions from books or papers: 30 min	
Fri	Transition elements: 20 min Electrode potentials and fuel cells: 10 min Lattice energy, ΔH and ΔS: 5 min K_c, K_p, pH and buffers: 1 min	Transition elements. Write summary notes and attempt questions from books or papers: 30 min	Reread (or rewrite) all of your summary notes
Sat	Transition elements: 10 min Electrode potentials and fuel cells: 5 min Lattice energy, ΔH and ΔS: 2 min K_c, K_p, pH and buffers: 1 min	Get someone to test you on your summary notes: 30 min	Try another past paper spread over two nights. List anything that you are unsure of and ask your teacher for help
Sun	Spend 5 min on each of the topics	Rewrite all of your summary notes: 30 min	

This revision timetable will give you an idea of how a timetable might work, but it is better for you to write one that will meet your needs. The important thing is that the grid at least enables you to see what you should be doing and when you should be doing it. Do not be too ambitious — little and often is the best way.

It would, of course, be more sensible to put together a longer rolling programme to cover all your A-level subjects. Try to work out a rolling programme that enables you to cover all your subjects over a 5–6-week period. Do *not* leave it too late. Start sooner rather than later.

Content Guidance

Module 5 builds on a number of different areas covered in year 1. It requires an understanding of reaction rates and chemical equilibrium from Module 3. It also extends your understanding of energetics and the calculations associated with it. Throughout this guide the essential pre-knowledge is outlined and references are made to the relevant year 1 modules.

Synoptic assessment

Module 5 examination papers contain questions that relate to principles first encountered in other modules and are designated synoptic questions. These questions relate the content of this module with knowledge and understanding acquired elsewhere in the course. You are expected to apply chemical principles from any part of the entire specification, including:

- mole calculations
- writing balanced equations
- empirical and molecular formula calculations
- bonding and structure

The content of this module is essentially quantitative and relates back to the corresponding qualitative chemistry in Module 3.

■ Rates, equilibrium and pH

How fast?

Experimental observations show that the rate of a reaction is influenced by temperature, concentration and the use of a catalyst.

The collision theory of reactivity helps to provide explanations for these observations. A reaction cannot take place unless a collision occurs between the reacting particles. Increasing temperature or concentration increases the chance of a collision occurring.

However, not all collisions lead to a successful reaction. The energy of a collision between reacting particles must exceed the minimum energy required to start the reaction. This minimum energy is known as the activation energy, E_a. Increasing the temperature affects the number of collisions with energy that exceeds E_a and the use of a catalyst affects the size of E_a.

Boltzmann distribution of molecular energies

Figure 1 shows a typical distribution of energies at constant temperature.

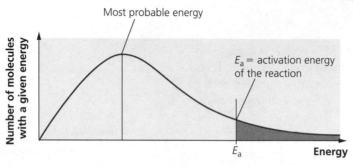

Figure 1

- The area under the curve represents the total number of particles.
- The shaded area represents the number of particles with energy greater than or equal to the activation energy, $E \geq E_a$ (showing the number of particles with sufficient energy to react).

Effect of concentration, temperature and catalyst on the rate of reaction

Concentration

Increasing concentration increases the chance of a collision. The more collisions there are, the faster the reaction will be.

For a gaseous reaction, increasing pressure has the same effect as increasing concentration. When gases react, they react faster at high pressure because there is an increased chance of a collision.

Temperature

An increase in temperature has a dramatic effect on the distribution of energies, as can be seen in Figure 2.

At higher temperatures the distribution flattens and shifts to the right such that:

- there are fewer particles with low energy
- the most probable energy moves to higher energy
- a greater proportion of particles have energy that exceeds the activation energy

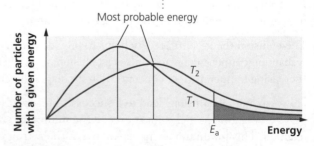

Figure 2

Increasing temperature increases the number of particles with energy greater than or equal to the activation energy, $E \geq E_a$, which means that at high temperatures there are more particles with sufficient energy to react and, therefore, the reaction is faster.

Catalyst

Catalysts work by lowering the activation energy for the reaction, which can be illustrated using an energy profile diagram and a Boltzmann distribution, as shown in Figure 3.

E_a is the activation energy of the uncatalysed reaction and E_{cat} is the activation energy of the catalysed reaction.

Module 5 builds on your understanding of the AS reaction rates chemistry. It involves measuring and calculating reaction rates using rate equations.

Reaction rate

The rate of a reaction is usually measured as the **change in concentration** of a reaction species **with time**.

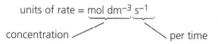

Measuring rates from graphs

For a reaction $A + B \rightarrow C + D$ it is possible to measure the rate of disappearance of either A or B, or the rate of appearance of one of the products, C or D.

- The rate of *decrease* in concentration of $A = -\dfrac{d[A]}{dt}$

- The rate of *increase* in concentration of $C = \dfrac{d[C]}{dt}$

The gradient of the concentration–time graph is a measure of the rate of a reaction (Figure 4).

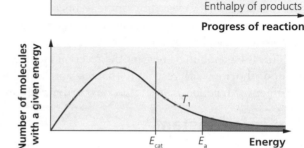

Figure 3

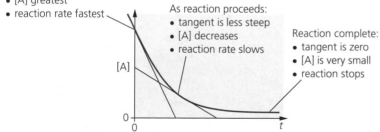

At start of reaction ($t = 0$):
- tangent is steepest
- [A] greatest
- reaction rate fastest

As reaction proceeds:
- tangent is less steep
- [A] decreases
- reaction rate slows

Reaction complete:
- tangent is zero
- [A] is very small
- reaction stops

Figure 4

Orders, rate equation and rate constants

Orders of reaction

The rate equation of a reaction shows how the rate is affected by concentrations of each reactant and can only be determined from experiments.

In general, for a reaction $A + B \rightarrow C + D$, the reaction rate is given by:

$$\text{rate} = k[A]^m[B]^n$$

where
- k is the rate constant of the reaction
- m and n are the **orders of reaction** with respect to A and B respectively
- the **overall order** of reaction is $(m + n)$

You know from Module 3 that increasing concentration usually results in an increased rate of reaction. However, different reagents can behave in a different manner. If we double the concentration of a reagent and the rate increases proportionately (that is, the rate also doubles) then the reaction is said to be **first order** with respect to that reagent. If by doubling a reagent the reaction increases four-fold, the reaction is said to **second order** with respect to that reagent, but if increasing the concentration has no effect the reaction is said to be **zero order** with respect to that reagent.

The rate constant

The rate constant, k, indicates the rate of the reaction:
- a large value of $k \rightarrow$ fast rate of reaction
- a small value of $k \rightarrow$ slow rate of reaction

An increase in temperature speeds up the rate of most reactions by *increasing* the rate constant, k.

Rate graphs and orders

During a reaction the concentrations of the reagents and of the products change and it is possible to measure concentration at regular intervals of time. The shape of the resultant graph can be used to predict the order of reaction.

Concentration–time graph

Zero-order reaction

The concentration falls at a steady rate with time (Figure 5).

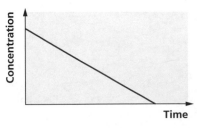

Figure 5

First-order reaction

The concentration halves in equal time periods (Figure 6). The shape of the graph indicates the order of the reaction by measuring the **half-life** of a reactant. The half-life of a reactant is the time required for its concentration to be reduced by half.

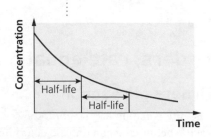

Figure 6

In a first-order reaction, rate = $k[X]$, if the half-life is known, or can be deduced from the graph, the rate constant, k, can be calculated by using the relationship:

$$k = \frac{\ln 2}{t_{1/2}}$$

($\ln 2$ is the natural logarithm of $2 = 0.693$)

($t_{1/2}$ is the half-life and can be measured from the graph)

Second-order reaction

The half-life becomes progressively longer as the reaction proceeds. The half-life *increases* with time (Figure 7).

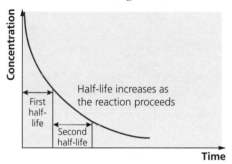

Figure 7

Rate–concentration graphs

A concentration–time graph is first plotted and tangents are drawn at several time values on the concentration–time graph, giving values of reaction rates. A second graph can now be plotted of rate against **concentration**.

Zero-order reaction

The rate is unaffected by changes in concentration (Figure 8).

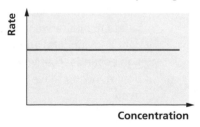

Figure 8

rate $\propto [X]^0$

So:

rate = constant

First-order reaction

If the concentration is doubled, the rate will also double (Figure 9).

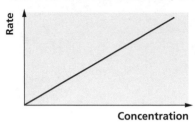

Figure 9

rate $\propto [X]^1$

Second-order reaction

If the concentration is doubled, the rate will increase four-fold (Figure 10).

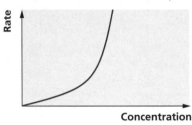

Figure 10

rate $\propto [X]^2$

The second-order relationship can be confirmed by plotting a graph of rate against $[X]^2$, which gives a straight line (Figure 11).

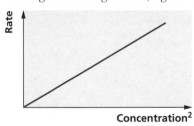

Figure 11

> **Exam tip**
>
> You are expected to know *two* sets of graphs, the shapes of which can be used to determine the order of reaction. One set plots concentration against time and the other shows the relationship between rate and concentration. It is essential that you do not mix up these graphs.

Measuring rates using the initial rates method

For a reaction, $A + B \rightarrow C + D$, carry out experiments using different initial concentrations of the reactants A and B.

Only change one variable at a time so two series of experiments will be required.

■ In series 1, the concentration of A is changed while the concentration of B is kept constant.

■ In series 2, the concentration of B is changed while the concentration of A is kept constant.

For each experiment plot a concentration–time graph and measure the initial rate from the graph of the tangent drawn at time = 0. A typical set of results looks like Table 1.

Table 1

Experiment	[A(aq)]/mol dm^{-3}	[B(aq)]/mol dm^{-3}	Initial rate/mol dm^{-3} s^{-1}
1	1.0×10^{-2}	1.0×10^{-2}	4.0×10^{-3}
2	2.0×10^{-2}	1.0×10^{-2}	1.6×10^{-2}
3	2.0×10^{-2}	2.0×10^{-2}	3.2×10^{-2}

Order of reaction with respect to each reagent

Order of reaction with respect to A

Comparing experiments 1 and 2, [B(aq)] is constant and [A(aq)] is varied. [A(aq)] has doubled, the rate has quadrupled, and the reaction is therefore second order with respect to A(aq), such that:

rate $\propto$ [A(aq)]^2

The concentration raised to the power 2 indicates that it is second order with respect to A(aq).

Order of reaction with respect to B

Comparing experiments 2 and 3, [A(aq)] is constant and [B(aq)] is varied. [B(aq)] has doubled, the rate doubles, and the reaction is therefore first order with respect to B(aq), such that:

rate $\propto$ [B(aq)]

The rate equation

Combining the two orders with respect to the two reagents gives:

rate $\propto$ [A(aq)]^2[B(aq)]

or

rate $= k$[A]^2[B]

and the overall order of this reaction is (2 + 1) = third order.

Rearranging the rate equation:

$$k = \frac{\text{rate}}{[A]^2[B]}$$

and substituting values from experiment 1, gives:

$$k = \frac{4.0 \times 10^{-3}}{(1.0 \times 10^{-2})(1.0 \times 10^{-2})}$$
$$= 40 \, \text{dm}^6 \, \text{mol}^{-2} \, \text{s}^{-1}$$

Knowledge check 1

For the rate equation; rate $= k$[A][B]^2, what will happen to the overall rate of reaction if **a** [A] is doubled, **b** [B] is halved, **c** both [A] and [B] are trebled?

Units of rate constants

The units of a rate constant depend on the rate equation for the reaction, as shown in Table 2.

Table 2

Order	Rate equation	Units of k
First	Rate = $k[A]$	s^{-1}
Second	Rate = $k[A]^2$	$dm^3\,mol^{-1}\,s^{-1}$
Third	Rate = $k[A]^2[B]$ or $k[A]^3$	$dm^6\,mol^{-2}\,s^{-1}$
Fourth	Rate = $k[A]^2[B]^2$	$dm^9\,mol^{-3}\,s^{-1}$

Knowledge check 2

What are the units of the rate constant, k, for **a** rate = $k[A][B]^2$ and **b** rate = $k[A]^2[B]^2[C]$?

Knowledge check 3

The table below gives data from the reaction:

$$BrO_3^- + 5Br^- + 6H^+ \rightarrow 3Br_2 + 3H_2O$$

The rate constant, $k = 8.2\,dm^9\,mol^{-3}\,s^{-1}$

$[BrO_3^-]/mol\,dm^{-3}$	$[Br^-]/mol\,dm^{-3}$	$[H^+]/mol\,dm^{-3}$	Initial rate $\times 10^{-3}/$ $mol\,dm^{-3}\,s^{-1}$
0.1	0.2	0.1	1.64
0.2	0.2	0.1	3.28
0.2	0.4	0.1	6.56

Deduce the order of reaction with respect to each reagent.

Continuous monitoring to determine reaction rate

A wide range of methods can be used and the method chosen will depend on the reaction under investigation.

- If a gas is evolved — the volume of gas could be measured at regular intervals of time.
- If the reaction involves acids or bases — the pH could be measured at regular intervals of time.
- If the reaction involves a colour change — a colorimeter could be used to monitor the change.

Rate-determining step

The **rate-determining step** is defined as the slowest step in the reaction.

The rate equation can provide clues about a likely reaction mechanism by identifying the slowest stage of a reaction sequence. For instance, if the rate equation is:

$$rate = k[A]^2[B]$$

the slow step will involve **2** mol of A and **1** mol of B, but if the rate equation is:

$$rate = k[A][B]^2$$

the slow step will involve **1** mol of A and **2** mol of B.

The orders in the rate equation match the number of species involved in the rate-determining step.

Reaction mechanisms often involve many separate steps. You may be asked to use the rate equation and the balanced equation to predict a mechanism that contains two steps. In a two-step mechanism, the rate equation indicates the number of moles of each reactant involved in the **slow** step.

slow step + the **fast** step = **balanced** equation

Example

For the reaction $2H_2(g) + 2NO(g) \rightarrow 2H_2O(l) + N_2(g)$, the rate equation is rate $= k[H_2(g)][NO(g)]^2$. Predict a two-step mechanism.

slow step	the rate equation tells us that this involves $1\,mol\,H_2(g)$ and $2\,mol\,NO(g)$

+

fast step

=

balanced equation	the balanced equation is given in the question. Just copy it down.

A possible two-step mechanism is:

slow step	$1H_2(g) + 2NO(g) \rightarrow H_2O(l) + N_2(g) + O(g)$

+

fast step	$1H_2(g) + O(g) \rightarrow H_2O(l)$

=

balanced equation	$2H_2(g) + 2NO(g) \rightarrow 2H_2O(l) + N_2(g)$

Effect of temperature on rate constants

In any reaction, if the concentrations of the reagents are unchanged, but the temperature is increased, the rate of reaction also increases. It follows that increasing the temperature must also increase the rate constant k. The relationship between the temperature and the rate constant is described in the Arrhenius equation.

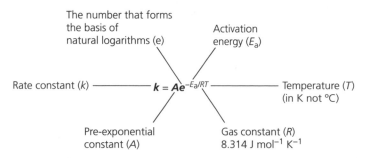

The number that forms the basis of natural logarithms (e)

Activation energy (E_a)

Rate constant (k) —— $k = Ae^{-E_a/RT}$ —— Temperature (T) (in K not °C)

Pre-exponential constant (A)

Gas constant (R) $8.314\,J\,mol^{-1}\,K^{-1}$

Exam tip

The slow step in any mechanism is usually the first step. The rate equation tells you the reagents and the number of moles of each reagent involved in the slow step. For example: in a reaction $2A + B + 2C \rightarrow 2X$, if the rate $= k[A][B]^2$ then the slow step involves $1\,mol$ of A, $2\,mol$ of B and no moles of C.

Knowledge check 4

Deduce a two-step mechanism for the reaction $2ICl + H_2 \rightarrow 2HCl + I_2$.

The rate equation is $r = k[ICl][H_2]$

If natural logarithms (ln) of the Arrhenius equation are taken, the equation can be written as:

$$\ln k = \ln A - \frac{E_a}{RT}$$

By plotting $\ln k$ against $1/T$ it should be possible to deduce values of the constant A and the activation energy E_a (Figure 12).

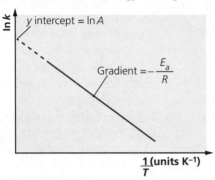

Figure 12

Exam tip

You will not be expected to remember this equation. It will be provided on the data sheet.

How far?

This follows on naturally from How fast? You should look back through the final section on chemical equilibrium in Module 3 (Periodic table and energy) in the second student guide of this series. This introduces the idea of a reversible reaction, a dynamic equilibrium and le Chatelier's principle and expression for K_c.

Before starting this section you should make sure that you can answer Knowledge checks 5, 6 and 7.

Knowledge check 5

Explain what is meant by each of the following:
- a reversible reaction
- a dynamic equilibrium
- le Chatelier's principle

Knowledge check 6

Sulfur trioxide, $SO_3(g)$, is an essential reagent in the production of sulfuric acid. It is obtained from the equilibrium:

$$2SO_2(g) + O_2(g) \rightleftharpoons 2SO_3(g) \qquad \Delta H = -196\,kJ\,mol^{-1}$$

Predict the optimum conditions in terms of temperature and pressure. Write an expression for K_c.

Knowledge check 7

Dinitrogen tetroxide, $N_2O_4(g)$, is a colourless gas, while nitrogen dioxide, NO_2, is a brown gas. The two gases exist in equilibrium:

$$N_2O_4(g) \rightleftharpoons 2NO_2(g) \qquad \Delta H = 58\,kJ\,mol^{-1}$$

a Write an expression for K_c.
b Explain what would be the effect on the equilibrium mixture of:
   i increasing temperature
   ii increasing pressure
   iii using a catalyst

In each case state what you would see.

The equilibrium constant, K_c

For year 2 chemistry, the exact position of equilibrium is calculated using the equilibrium law.

The equilibrium law

K_c is the equilibrium constant in terms of equilibrium concentrations. The equilibrium law states that, for an equation:

$$aA + bB \rightleftharpoons cC + dD$$

$$K_c = \frac{[C]^c[D]^d}{[A]^a[B]^b}$$

- [A], [B], [C] and [D] are the **equilibrium** concentrations of the reactants and products in the reaction.
- Each product and reactant has its equilibrium concentration raised to the **power** of its **balancing number** (a, b etc.) in the equation.

Working out K_c

For the equilibrium $H_2(g) + I_2(g) \rightleftharpoons 2HI(g)$, applying the equilibrium law gives:

$$K_c = \frac{[HI(g)]^2}{[H_2(g)][I_2(g)]}$$

At equilibrium, $[H_2(g)] = 0.012\,mol\,dm^{-3}$, $[I_2(g)] = 0.001\,mol\,dm^{-3}$, and $[HI(g)] = 0.025\,mol\,dm^{-3}$.

$$K_c = \frac{[HI(g)]^2}{[H_2(g)][I_2(g)]}$$

$$= \frac{0.025^2}{0.012 \times 0.001} = 52.1$$

Units of K_c

The units of K_c are dependent upon the equilibrium expression for the reaction. Each concentration value is replaced by its units:

$$K_c = \frac{[HI(g)]^2}{[H_2(g)][I_2(g)]} = \frac{(mol\,dm^{-3})^2}{(mol\,dm^{-3})(mol\,dm^{-3})}$$

For this equilibrium, the units cancel and K_c has no units.

Writing expressions for K_c

It is essential that you are able to write expressions for K_c and are to be able to deduce the units, if any, for each expression.

	Equilibrium		
	$2NO_2(g) \rightleftharpoons N_2O_4(g)$	$N_2(g) + 3H_2(g) \rightleftharpoons 2NH_3(g)$	$Br_2(g) + H_2(g) \rightleftharpoons 2HBr(g)$
K_c	$\dfrac{[N_2O_4(g)]}{[NO_2(g)]^2}$	$\dfrac{[NH_3(g)]^2}{[N_2(g)][H_2(g)]^3}$	$\dfrac{[HBr(g)]^2}{[H_2(g)][Br_2(g)]}$
Units	$mol^{-1}\,dm^3$	$mol^{-2}\,dm^6$	None

Knowledge check 8

What are the units of K_c for:

a $PCl_3(g) + Cl_2(g) \rightleftharpoons PCl_5(g)$ and

b $2SO_2(g) + O_2(g) \rightleftharpoons 2SO_3(g)$?

Exam tip

When calculating a value for K_c, first check the units. If there are no units it does not matter whether you use moles or concentrations of each chemical. For a reaction such as $2NO_2(g) \rightleftharpoons N_2O_4(g)$ it is necessary to convert the moles of gas into concentrations before calculating K_c.

In an **exothermic** reaction, K_c *decreases* with increasing temperature because raising the temperature reduces the equilibrium yield of products.

In an **endothermic** reaction, K_c *increases* with increasing temperature because raising the temperature increases the equilibrium yield of products.

Determination of K_c from experiment

The equilibrium constant, K_c, can be determined from experimental results.

Example

This example illustrates how to answer a typical question.

0.200 mol CH_3COOH and 0.100 mol C_2H_5OH were mixed together with a trace of acid catalyst in a total volume of 200 cm³. The mixture was allowed to reach equilibrium:

$$CH_3COOH + C_2H_5OH \rightleftharpoons CH_3COOC_2H_5 + H_2O$$

Analysis of the mixture showed that 0.115 mol of CH_3COOH were present at equilibrium. Calculate the equilibrium constant, K_c.

Answer

From the information given, the number of moles of CH_3COOH that reacted = 0.200 − 0.115 = 0.085. The balanced equation tells us the molar ratio of the reactants and the products:

Balanced equation	CH_3COOH	+ C_2H_5OH	$\rightleftharpoons$ $CH_3COOC_2H_5$	+ H_2O
Molar ratio	1 mol	1 mol	$\rightarrow$ 1 mol	1 mol
Change/mol	−0.085	−0.085	+0.085	+0.085

	CH_3COOH	+ C_2H_5OH	$\rightleftharpoons$ $CH_3COOC_2H_5$	+ H_2O
Initial amount/mol	0.200	0.100	0	0
Change in moles	−0.085	−0.085	+0.085	+0.085
Equilibrium amount/mol	0.115	0.015	0.085	0.085
Equilibrium concentration/ mol dm⁻³	0.115/0.20	0.015/0.20	0.085/0.20	0.085/0.20

Write the expression for K_c, substitute values and calculate K_c:

$$K_c = \frac{[CH_3COOC_2H_5][H_2O]}{[CH_3COOH][C_2H_5OH]}$$

$$= \frac{\left(\dfrac{0.085}{0.20}\right) \times \left(\dfrac{0.085}{0.20}\right)}{\left(\dfrac{0.115}{0.20}\right) \times \left(\dfrac{0.015}{0.20}\right)} = \frac{0.425 \times 0.425}{0.575 \times 0.075} = 4.19$$

The answer does not have any units because they all cancel.

Knowledge check 9

$N_2(g)$ and $H_2(g)$ were mixed in a 4.0 dm³ container and allowed to reach equilibrium. The equilibrium mixture contained 5.0 mol $N_2(g)$, 10.0 mol $H_2(g)$ and 5.0 mol $NH_3(g)$. Calculate K_c for $N_2(g) + 3H_2(g) \rightleftharpoons 2NH_3(g)$.

Knowledge check 10

0.4 mol $H_2(g)$ and 0.3 mol $I_2(g)$ were mixed in a 2 dm³ flask and allowed to reach equilibrium. The equilibrium mixture contained 0.2 mol HI(g). Deduce the amount of H_2 and I_2 in the equilibrium mixture and calculate K_c for $H_2(g) + I_2(g) \rightleftharpoons 2HI(g)$.

The equilibrium constant, K_p

If an equilibrium involves just gases it is normal to measure pressure rather than concentration, and the equilibrium constant is K_p rather than K_c.

The pressure of a gas depends on the amount in moles of the gas in a given volume.

For a mixture of gases, the pressure of an individual gas within the mixture is directly related to its **mole fraction**.

> The **mole fraction** is the amount in moles of the gas divided by the total amount, in moles, of all the gases in the mixture.
>
> $$\text{mole fraction} = \frac{\text{moles of gas}}{\text{total moles of all gases}}$$

In a mixture of gases the pressure contributed by an individual gas is called the **partial pressure** of that gas. The partial pressure of all the gases in a mixture must add up to the total pressure of that mixture.

The total pressure is then the sum of the individual pressures contributed by each gas. Since the mole is a measure of a number of particles, the overall pressure of a mixture depends on the sum of the amount in moles of each gas present.

So for gases an equilibrium constant, K_p, is defined based on the pressure that each individual component gas is contributing to the overall pressure.

This pressure of each component gas is known as its **partial pressure**.

> The **partial pressure** is the pressure that would be exerted by a gas in a mixture of gases if it occupied the same volume on its own at the same temperature.

> The partial pressure of each gas in a mixture can be calculated by using:
>
> $$\begin{array}{c}\text{partial pressure of gas A} \\ \text{in a mixture of gases}\end{array} = \begin{array}{c}\text{mole fraction} \\ \text{of gas A}\end{array} \times \begin{array}{c}\text{total pressure of} \\ \text{gas mixture}\end{array}$$

Writing expressions for K_p

It is essential that you are able to write expressions for K_p and are able to deduce the units, if any, for each expression. For the reaction:

$$a\text{W(g)} + b\text{X(g)} \rightleftharpoons c\text{Y(g)} + d\text{Z(g)}$$

the expression for K_p is:

$$K_p = \frac{P_Y{}^c \times P_Z{}^d}{P_W{}^a \times P_X{}^b}$$

	Equilibrium		
	$2NO_2(g) \rightleftharpoons N_2O_4(g)$	$N_2(g) + 3H_2(g) \rightleftharpoons 2NH_3(g)$	$Br_2(g) + H_2(g) \rightleftharpoons 2HBr(g)$
K_p	$\dfrac{P_{N_2O_4}}{P^2{}_{NO_2}}$	$\dfrac{P^2{}_{NH_3}}{P_{H_2} \times P^3{}_{N_2}}$	$\dfrac{P^2{}_{HBr}}{P_{H_2} \times P_{Br_2}}$
Units	kPa^{-1}	kPa^{-2}	None

Exam tip

The mole fractions of all the gases in a mixture *must* always add up to 1.

Knowledge check 11

A mixture of three gases A, B and C has a total pressure of 200 kPa. The mixture contains 0.1 mol gas A, 0.4 mol gas B and 0.6 mol gas C. Calculate:

a the mole fraction of each gas

b the partial pressure of each gas

Knowledge check 12

State the units of K_p for:

a $PCl_3(g) + Cl_2(g) \rightleftharpoons$
$PCl_5(g)$

b $2SO_2(g) + O_2(g) \rightleftharpoons$
$2SO_3(g)$

Properties of K_c and K_p

K_c and K_p indicate how *far* a reaction proceeds but tell us nothing about how *fast* the reaction occurs. The size of *equilibrium constants* indicates the extent of a chemical equilibrium.

If K_c or K_p is large (e.g. $K_c = 1000$) the equilibrium lies to the right-hand side and there will be a high percentage of product formed.

If K_c or K_p is small (e.g. $K_p = 1 \times 10^{-3}$) the equilibrium lies to the left-hand side and there will be a low percentage of product formed.

If K_c or $K_p = 1$ the equilibrium lies half way between reactants and products.

Changing K_c and K_p

Both K_c and K_p are constants *but* both are temperature dependent. They are unaffected by changes in concentration or pressure but both can be changed by altering the temperature.

It is easy to see why changing a concentration does not change K_c, but more difficult when considering a change in pressure.

In the Haber process, $N_2(g) + 3H_2(g) \rightleftharpoons 2NH_3(g)$, le Chatelier's principle predicts that an increase in pressure moves the equilibrium to the right, which is true. If nothing else happened the value of K_c would increase. However, increasing pressure also decreases the volume, which changes the concentrations. This change in concentrations ensures that K_c remains constant.

Acids, bases and buffers

Acids were introduced in year 1. You should be able to define an acid as a proton donor and be able to write equations for the reactions of acids. You should also be able to write full and ionic equations for the reactions of acids with metals, metal oxides, hydroxides and carbonates.

An acid–base reaction involves proton transfer:

$NaOH(aq) + HCl(aq) \rightarrow NaCl(aq) + H_2O(l)$

which can be simplified to:

$H^+(aq) + OH^-(aq) \rightarrow H_2O(l)$

Acids also react with carbonates:

$Na_2CO_3(aq) + 2HCl(aq) \rightarrow 2NaCl(aq) + CO_2(g) + H_2O(l)$

giving the ionic equation:

$CO_3^{2-}(aq) + 2H^+(aq) \rightarrow CO_2(g) + H_2O(l)$

In this case the acid donates protons to the carbonate, which splits into carbon dioxide and water. The carbonate is therefore a base in the reaction.

Acids also react with metal oxides (bases):

$MgO(s) + 2HCl(aq) \rightarrow MgCl_2(aq) + H_2O(l)$

Knowledge check 13

At 500 K the following equilibrium is formed:

$PCl_5(g) \rightleftharpoons PCl_3(g) + Cl_2(g)$

In an experiment 0.15 mol of PCl_5 was heated to 500 K and allowed to reach equilibrium. It was found to contain 0.10 mol of PCl_3 and the total pressure was 110 kPa. Calculate K_p.

Exam tip

In an equation the state symbol (aq) usually indicates that the compound is ionic and that the ions are mobile. So usually, in an ionic equation, any compound with the state symbol (aq) should be written as separate ions.

giving the ionic equation:

$$MgO(s) + 2H^+(aq) \rightarrow Mg^{2+}(aq) + H_2O(l)$$

$MgO(s)$ is ionic but in the solid form the ions are not free to move so $MgO(s)$ is not written as separate ions.

Conjugate acid–base pairs

A molecule of an acid contains a hydrogen that can be released as a positive hydrogen ion or proton, H^+.

Acids and bases are linked by H^+ as **conjugate pairs**, such that the **conjugate acid** donates H^+ and the **conjugate base** accepts H^+. An acid can only donate a proton if there is a base to accept it. By mixing an acid with a base, an equilibrium is set up between *two* acid–base **conjugate pairs** (Figure 13).

In the forward reaction:
- $CH_3COOH(aq)$ donates a H^+ to the water and therefore behaves as an acid
- H_2O accepts a H^+ from $CH_3COOH(aq)$ and therefore behaves as a base

$$CH_3COOH(aq) \quad + \quad H_2O(l) \quad \rightleftharpoons \quad H_3O^+ \quad + \quad CH_3COO^-(aq)$$

In the reverse reaction:
- H_3O^+ donates a H^+ to the $CH_3COO^-(aq)$ and therefore behaves as an acid
- $CH_3COO^-(aq)$ accepts a H^+ from H_3O^+ and therefore behaves as a base

Figure 13

$CH_3COOH(aq)$ and $CH_3COO^-(aq)$ form an acid–base conjugate pair and H_3O^+ and $H_2O(l)$ form a second acid–base conjugate pair.

In the equilibrium $NH_3(g) + H_2O(l) \rightleftharpoons NH_4^+(aq) + OH^-(aq)$ it can be seen that, in the forward reaction, the water has donated a proton to the ammonia and is therefore the acid while the ammonia is the base. For the reverse reaction the ammonium ion is the acid and the hydroxide is the base.

In summary:

$$NH_3(g) \quad + \quad H_2O(l) \quad \rightleftharpoons \quad NH_4^+(aq) \quad + \quad OH^-(aq)$$

Base 2   **Acid 1**   **Acid 2**   **Base 1**

Monobasic, dibasic and tribasic acids

Acids are proton donors and acids such as HCl, HNO_3 and CH_3COOH contain only one acidic proton and are therefore *monobasic* and only form one salt. Sulfuric acid contains two acidic protons and can react with a base to form two different salts:

$$H_2SO_4 + NaOH \rightarrow NaHSO_4 + H_2O \text{ (a hydrogensulfate salt is formed)}$$

$$H_2SO_4 + 2NaOH \rightarrow Na_2SO_4 + 2H_2O \text{ (a sulfate salt is formed)}$$

H_2SO_4 is therefore *dibasic*.

HARROW COLLEGE
Learning Centre

Knowledge check 14

Deduce the formula of the salt formed from each of the following acid–base reactions:
a $CH_3COOH + KOH$
b $HCOOH + Mg(OH)_2$
c $H_3PO_4 + CaCO_3$

An acid–base **conjugate pair** is linked together by H^+; the **conjugate acid** donates H^+ and the **conjugate base** accepts H^+.

Knowledge check 15

Identify the conjugate **base** for each of the following: **a** H_2O, **b** HSO_4^-, **c** NH_3, **d** C_6H_5COOH.

Knowledge check 16

Identify the conjugate **acid** for each of the following: **a** H_2O, **b** HSO_4^-, **c** NH_3, **d** CH_3NH_2.

Phosphoric acid has three acidic protons and is therefore *tribasic* and can form three different salts:

$H_3PO_4 + NaOH \rightarrow NaH_2PO_4 + H_2O$ (a dihydrogenphosphate salt is formed)

$H_3PO_4 + 2NaOH \rightarrow Na_2HPO_4 + 2H_2O$ (a hydrogenphosphate salt is formed)

$H_3PO_4 + 3NaOH \rightarrow Na_3PO_4 + 3H_2O$ (a phosphate salt is formed)

Strengths of acids and bases

The acid–base equilibrium of an acid, HA, in water is:

$$HA(aq) + H_2O(l) \rightleftharpoons H_3O^+(aq) + A^-(aq)$$

or, to emphasise the loss of a proton, H^+, by dissociation:

$$HA(aq) \rightleftharpoons H^+(aq) + A^-(aq)$$

The strength of an acid shows the extent of dissociation into H^+ and A^-.

Strong acids

Acids vary considerably in the ease with which they are able to release their hydrogen ions. A strong acid, such as nitric acid, HNO_3, is a good proton donor, for which the equilibrium position is well to the right:

$$\xrightarrow{\text{equilibrium}}$$
$$HNO_3(aq) \rightleftharpoons H^+(aq) + NO_3^-(aq)$$

There is almost complete dissociation and it is usual to write the equation as:

$$HNO_3(aq) \rightarrow H^+(aq) + NO_3^-(aq)$$

Weak acids

A weak acid, such as ethanoic acid, CH_3COOH, is a poor proton donor with the equilibrium position well to the left.

$$\xleftarrow{\text{equilibrium}}$$
$$CH_3COOH(aq) \rightleftharpoons H^+(aq) + CH_3COO^-(aq)$$

There is only partial dissociation.

It is important to distinguish between the terms 'strong' and 'concentrated'.

A **strong** acid is one that is highly ionised in aqueous solution. A **concentrated** acid is one made by dissolving large amounts of the acid in a small volume of water.

A **weak** acid is one that is only partially ionised in aqueous solution. A **dilute** acid is one made by dissolving small amounts of the acid in a large volume of water.

The usual way of indicating the strength of an acid is to use the equilibrium constant for its ionisation in water.

The acid dissociation constant, K_a

The extent of acid dissociation is shown by an equilibrium constant called the **acid dissociation constant**, K_a, where the subscript 'a' indicates that the reaction involves an acid.

Exam tip

To illustrate acid–base conjugate pairs, questions may use two acids — one strong and one weak. Remember that the stronger acid (the acid with the lower pH or pK_a value) will donate a proton to the weaker acid.

Knowledge check 17

Ethanoic acid is mixed with nitric acid, forming an equilibrium containing acid–base conjugate pairs. Complete the following equation:

$CH_3CO_2H + HNO_3$
$\rightleftharpoons$ .... +
....

For the reaction $HA(aq) \rightleftharpoons H^+(aq) + A^-(aq)$

$$K_a = \frac{[H^+(aq)][A^-(aq)]}{[HA(aq)]}$$

The units are:

$$K_a = \frac{[(mol\,dm^{-3})^2]}{(mol\,dm^{-3})} = mol\,dm^{-3}$$

A **large** K_a value indicates that the acid is a strong acid.

A **small** K_a value indicates that the acid is weak acid.

Ethanoic acid ionises as:

$$CH_3COOH(aq) \rightleftharpoons CH_3COO^-(aq) + H^+(aq)$$

As with the other equilibria, an equilibrium constant can be defined for this reaction as:

$$K_a = \frac{[CH_3COO^-(aq)][H^+(aq)]}{[CH_3COOH(aq)]}$$

For ethanoic acid K_a has a value of 1.7×10^{-5}, which makes it clear that a solution of ethanoic acid consists largely of ethanoic acid molecules with only relatively few ethanoate ions and hydrogen ions.

Methanoic acid has a K_a value of 1.6×10^{-4}, which is almost ten times larger than the figure for ethanoic acid. This tells us that methanoic acid, though weak, is stronger than ethanoic acid.

The mineral acids have much larger values for K_a. Nitric acid, for example, is approximately 40, and sulfuric acid is often listed with just the comment 'very large'.

Calculating hydrogen ion concentrations

The pH scale

The concentrations of $H^+(aq)$ ions in acid solutions vary widely between about $10\,mol\,dm^{-3}$ and about $1 \times 10^{-15}\,mol\,dm^{-3}$. The **pH** scale (Figure 14) is used to overcome the problem of these small numbers. This is a logarithmic scale, such that each change of 1 on the pH scale corresponds to a ten-fold change in the $[H^+(aq)]$.

pH	0	1	2	3	4	5	6	7	8	9	10	11	12	13	14
$[H^+]$	1	10^{-1}	10^{-2}	10^{-3}	10^{-4}	10^{-5}	10^{-6}	10^{-7}	10^{-8}	10^{-9}	10^{-10}	10^{-11}	10^{-12}	10^{-13}	10^{-14}

More acidic ← ———————— Neutral ———————— → More alkaline

Figure 14

You should be able to convert between pH and $H^+(aq)$ and vice versa using the relationships below:

$$pH = -\log_{10}[H^+(aq)]$$

and

$$[H^+(aq)] = 10^{-pH}$$

pH is defined by the equation:
$$pH = -\log[H^+(aq)]$$

Knowledge check 18

a Calculate the pH of each of the following solutions with $[H^+]$ concentrations of
  i $0.01\,mol\,dm^{-3}$
  ii $0.05\,mol\,dm^{-3}$
  iii $1.50 \times 10^{-6}\,mol\,dm^{-3}$
b Calculate the $[H^+]$ concentration of each of the following solutions with a pH of
  i 6.45, **ii** 3.25, **iii** 1.25.

Calculating the pH of strong acids

For a strong acid, we can assume **complete dissociation** and the concentration of $H^+(aq)$ can be found from the acid concentration.

Example 1

A strong acid, HA, has a concentration of $0.020\,mol\,dm^{-3}$. What is the pH?

Answer

There is complete dissociation, therefore $[H^+(aq)] = 0.020\,mol\,dm^{-3}$, and:

$$pH = -\log_{10}[H^+(aq)]$$

$$= -\log_{10}0.020 = 1.7$$

Example 2

A strong acid, HA, has a pH of 2.4. What is the concentration of $H^+(aq)$?

Answer

There is complete dissociation, therefore $[H^+(aq)] = 10^{-pH} = 10^{-2.4}\,mol\,dm^{-3}$, so:

$$[H^+(aq)] = 3.98 \times 10^{-3}\,mol\,dm^{-3}$$

Knowledge check 19

Calculate the pH of:
a $0.1\,mol\,dm^{-3}$ HCl(aq)
b $0.01\,mol\,dm^{-3}$ HCl(aq)
c $0.001\,mol\,dm^{-3}$ HCl(aq)

Calculating the pH of weak acids

To calculate the pH of a strong acid all that you need to know is the concentration of the strong acid. Weak acids do not completely dissociate so to calculate the pH of a weak acid, HA, you need to know:

- the concentration of the acid
- the acid dissociation constant, K_a

In the equilibrium of a weak aqueous acid, $HA(aq) \rightleftharpoons H^+(aq) + A^-(aq)$, we assume that:

- only a very small proportion of HA dissociates and hence the amount of undissociated acid is the same as the initial concentration of $[HA(aq)]$
- there is a negligible proportion of $H^+(aq)$ from ionisation of water, such that $[H^+(aq)] = [A^-(aq)]$

Using these approximations:

$$K_a = \frac{[H^+(aq)][A^-(aq)]}{[HA(aq)]} \approx \frac{[H^+(aq)]^2}{[HA(aq)]}$$

Example

For a weak acid, $[HA (aq)] = 0.200 \, mol \, dm^{-3}$, and $K_a = 1.70 \times 10^{-4} \, mol \, dm^{-3}$ at 25°C. Calculate the pH.

Answer

$$K_a = \frac{[H^+(aq)][A^-(aq)]}{[HA(aq)]} \approx \frac{[H^+(aq)]^2}{[HA(aq)]}$$

Therefore:

$$1.70 \times 10^{-4} = \frac{[H^+(aq)]^2}{0.200}$$

$$1.70 \times 10^{-4} \times 0.200 = [H^+(aq)]^2$$

$$[H^+(aq)] = \sqrt{1.70 \times 10^{-4} \times 0.200}$$

$$= 5.83 \times 10^{-3} = 0.00583$$

$$pH = -\log_{10}[H^+(aq)]$$

$$= -\log_{10} 0.00583 = 2.23$$

An alternative way of doing this type of calculation is to use the equation:

$$pH = -\log_{10}\sqrt{(K_a \text{ of HA}) \times (\text{concentration of HA})}$$

or

$$pH = -\log_{10}\sqrt{K_a \times [HA]}$$

The same calculation can now be carried out in a single step:

$$pH = -\log_{10}\sqrt{1.70 \times 10^{-4} \times 0.200}$$

$$= 2.23$$

K_a and pK_a

As with $[H^+(aq)]$ and pH, K_a is often expressed in a logarithmic form, pK_a, which is defined as:

$$pK_a = -\log_{10}K_a$$

With this logarithmic scale, each change of 1 on the pK_a scale corresponds to a ten-fold change in the K_a (Table 3). Like pH, pK_a can be used as a guide to the acidity. The lower the pK_a value the stronger the acid.

Table 3

Acid		K_a/mol dm^{-3}	pK_a
Ethanoic acid	CH_3COOH	1.7×10^{-5}	$-\log_{10}(1.7 \times 10^{-5}) = 4.77$
Benzoic acid	C_6H_5COOH	6.3×10^{-5}	$-\log_{10}(6.3 \times 10^{-5}) = 4.20$

This indicates that benzoic acid is a stronger acid than ethanoic acid.

Knowledge check 20

The K_a values of three acids A, B and C are:
A = $7.70 \times 10^{-4} \, mol \, dm^{-3}$
B = $6.60 \times 10^{-3} \, mol \, dm^{-3}$
C = $4.20 \times 10^{-4} \, mol \, dm^{-3}$
Put the acids in order of strength starting with the strongest acid.

Exam tip

This method used in the example has limitations when calculating the pH of *stronger* weak acids. The calculation described in the example assumes that the concentration of the undissociated acid remains the same, which would not be the case with *stronger* weak acids.

pK_a is defined by the equation:
$pK_a = -\log_{10}(K_a)$

Knowledge check 21

Use the data in the Table 3 to calculate how much stronger benzoic acid is than ethanoic acid.

The ionic product of water, K_w

Water ionises very slightly, acting as both an acid and a base:

$H_2O(l)$	$+$ $H_2O(l)$	$\rightleftharpoons$	$H_3O^+(aq)$	$+$ $OH^-(aq)$
Acid 1	Base 2		Acid 2	Base 1
(donates proton)	(accepts proton)		(donates proton)	(accepts proton)

or, more simply:

$$\xleftarrow{\text{equilibrium}}$$

$$H_2O(l) \rightleftharpoons H^+(aq) + OH^-(aq)$$

In water, a very small proportion of molecules dissociates into $H^+(aq)$ and $OH^-(aq)$ ions. Treating water as a weak acid:

$$K_a = \frac{[H^+(aq)][OH^-(aq)]}{[H_2O(l)]}$$

Rearranging gives:

$$\underbrace{K_a \times [H_2O(l)]}_{\text{constant, } K_w} = [H^+(aq)][OH^-(aq)]$$

K_w is called the **ionic product** of water:

$$K_w = [H^+(aq)][OH^-(aq)] = 1.0 \times 10^{-14}\,\text{mol}^2\,\text{dm}^{-6} \text{ (at 25°C).}$$

K_w is temperature dependent and is only equal to $1.0 \times 10^{-14}\,\text{mol}^2\,\text{dm}^{-6}$ at 25°C (298 K).

At 10°C (283 K), $K_w = 2.9 \times 10^{-15}\,\text{mol}^2\,\text{dm}^{-6}$, while at 40°C (313 K), $K_w = 2.9 \times 10^{-14}\,\text{mol}^2\,\text{dm}^{-6}$.

Using K_w to calculate the pH of water

At 25°C $K_w = [H^+(aq)][OH^-(aq)] = 1.0 \times 10^{-14}\,\text{mol}^2\,\text{dm}^{-6}$.
Assume that $[H^+(aq)] = [OH^-(aq)]$, such that $K_w = [H^+(aq)]^2 = 1.0 \times 10^{-14}\,\text{mol}^2\,\text{dm}^{-6}$:

$$[H^+(aq)] = 1.0 \times 10^{-7}\,\text{mol}^2\,\text{dm}^{-6}$$

$$pH = -\log_{10}[H^+(aq)] = -\log_{10}(1.0 \times 10^{-7}) = 7$$

Using K_w to calculate the pH of strong alkalis

The pH of a strong alkali, such as NaOH, can be calculated from the concentration of the alkali and the ionic product of water, K_w.

Exam tip

When carrying out calculations it is important not to round numbers until the end of the calculation. Make sure that you know how to store numbers in your calculator.

Knowledge check 22

The ionisation product, K_w, for $H_2O(l)$ $\rightleftharpoons H^+(aq) + OH^-(aq)$ is temperature dependent. At 25°C, $K_w = 1.0 \times 10^{-14}\,\text{mol}\,\text{dm}^{-3}$; at 50°C, $K_w = 5.6 \times 10^{-4}\,\text{mol}^2\,\text{dm}^{-6}$. Deduce the sign of ΔH for $H_2O(l)$ $\rightleftharpoons H^+(aq) + OH^-(aq)$.

Knowledge check 23

Example

A strong alkali, KOH, has a concentration of $0.50\,mol\,dm^{-3}$. What is the pH at $25°C$?

Answer

$KOH(aq) \rightarrow K^+(aq) + OH^-(aq)$ and since the dissociation is complete:

$[OH^-(aq)] = [KOH(aq)] = 0.50\,mol\,dm^{-3}$

First find $[H^+]$ using K_w and $[OH^-]$:

$$K_w = [H^+(aq)][OH^-(aq)] = 1 \times 10^{-14}\,mol^2\,dm^{-6}$$

Therefore:

$$[H^+(aq)] = \frac{K_w}{[OH^-(aq)]} = \frac{1 \times 10^{-14}}{0.50} = 2 \times 10^{-13}\,mol\,dm^{-3}$$

$$pH = -\log_{10}[H^+(aq)] = -\log_{10}(2 \times 10^{-13}) = 12.7$$

Calculate the pH of each of the following aqueous solutions:
a $0.15\,mol\,dm^{-3}$ HNO_3
b $0.15\,mol\,dm^{-3}$ HCN ($K_a = 4.8 \times 10^{-10}\,mol\,dm^{-3}$)
c $0.15\,mol\,dm^{-3}$ NaOH
d a mixture of $20\,cm^3$ of $1.0\,mol\,dm^{-3}$ HCl and $10\,cm^3$ of $1.0\,mol\,dm^{-3}$ NaOH

Buffer solutions

A **buffer solution** is a solution that 'resists' changes in pH during the addition of small amounts of an acid or an alkali.

Making a buffer solution

A buffer solution is a mixture of a weak acid, HA, and its conjugate base, A^-:

$$HA(aq) \rightleftharpoons H^+(aq) + A^-(aq)$$
weak acid $\qquad$ conjugate base

An example of a common buffer solution is a mixture of CH_3COOH (the weak acid) and $CH_3COO^-Na^+$ (the conjugate base) (Figure 15). A mixture of any weak acid and the salt of that weak acid can be used as a buffer. The pH at which the buffer operates depends on the K_a of the weak acid and the relative concentrations of the weak acid and the conjugate base.

A mixture of CH_3COOH and $CH_3COO^-Na^+$:

$CH_3COOH(aq) \rightleftharpoons CH_3COO^-(aq) + H^+(aq)$ — This only partially dissociates giving low concentrations of $CH_3COO^-(aq)$ and $H^+(aq)$

$CH_3COO^-Na^+(aq) \rightarrow CH_3COO^-(aq) + Na^+(aq)$ — This totally dissociates giving high concentrations of $CH_3COO^-(aq)$

Figure 15

The high $[CH_3COO^-(aq)]$ forces the equilibrium back to the left-hand side and results in the buffer solution containing very low $[H^+(aq)]$ and very high $[CH_3COOH(aq)]$ and $[CH_3COO^-(aq)]$. The high concentrations of $[CH_3COOH(aq)]$ and $[CH_3COO^-(aq)]$ resist any changes in pH.

A **buffer solution** is a solution that resists changes in pH during the addition of an acid or an alkali and maintains a near constant pH by removing most of the added acid or alkali.

Exam tip

Many buffers are prepared by mixing together a weak acid and a strong base — the weak acid *must* be in excess. For example, when $100\,cm^3$ of $0.2\,mol\,dm^{-3}$ $CH_3COOH(aq)$ is mixed with $100\,cm^3$ of $0.1\,mol\,dm^{-3}$ $NaOH(aq)$, the resultant mixture contains unreacted $CH_3COOH(aq)$ and its salt $CH_3COO^-Na^+(aq)$, which are the essential components of the buffer.

How does a buffer act?

A buffer solution contains three important components:

■ high concentration of the weak acid $CH_3COOH(aq)$
■ high concentration of the conjugate base $CH_3COO^-(aq)$
■ low concentration of $H^+(aq)$

On addition of an acid, $H^+(aq)$, the high concentration of the conjugate base, $CH_3COO^-(aq)$, removes most of the added $H^+(aq)$ by forming $CH_3COOH(aq)$:

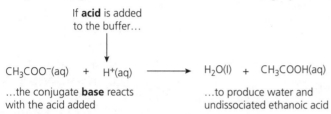

If **acid** is added
to the buffer…

$$CH_3COO^-(aq) \quad + \quad H^+(aq) \longrightarrow H_2O(l) \quad + \quad CH_3COOH(aq)$$

…the conjugate **base** reacts
with the acid added

…to produce water and
undissociated ethanoic acid

On addition of an alkali, $OH^-(aq)$, the high concentration of $CH_3COOH(aq)$ removes most of the added $OH^-(aq)$ by forming $CH_3COO^-(aq)$:

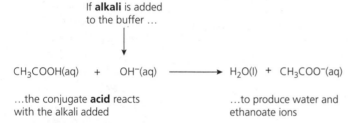

If **alkali** is added
to the buffer …

$$CH_3COOH(aq) \quad + \quad OH^-(aq) \longrightarrow H_2O(l) \quad + \quad CH_3COO^-(aq)$$

…the conjugate **acid** reacts
with the alkali added

…to produce water and
ethanoate ions

A buffer cannot cancel out the effect of any acid or alkali that is added. The buffer removes most of any acid or alkali that is added and *minimises* any changes in pH.

Calculations involving buffer solutions

The pH of a buffer solution depends upon the acid dissociation constant, K_a, of the buffer system and the ratios of the weak acid and its conjugate base.

For a buffer containing the weak acid, HA, and its conjugate base, the salt A^-:

$$K_a = \frac{[salt][H^+]}{[acid]}$$

which can be arranged to give:

$$K_a \frac{[acid]}{[salt]} = [H^+]$$

Remember that $pH = -\log_{10}[H^+]$. Therefore:

$$pH = -\log_{10}K_a \frac{[acid]}{[salt]}$$

It follows that the pH of a buffer can be changed by altering the ratio of the weak acid to the conjugate base.

Example

a Calculate the pH of a buffer with concentrations of $0.10 \, \text{mol} \, \text{dm}^{-3}$ $CH_3COOH(aq)$ and $0.10 \, \text{mol} \, \text{dm}^{-3}$ $CH_3COO^-(aq)$.

b What happens to the pH if the concentration of $CH_3COOH(aq)$ is changed to $0.30 \, \text{mol} \, \text{dm}^{-3}$ CH_3COOH?
$K_a = 1.7 \times 10^{-5} \, \text{mol} \, \text{dm}^{-3}$

Answer

a First calculate $[H^+(aq)]$ using:

$$[H^+(aq)] = K_a \times \frac{[HA(aq)]}{[A^-(aq)]}$$

$$[H^+(aq)] = \frac{1.7 \times 10^{-5} \times 0.10}{0.10}$$

$$[H^+(aq)] = 1.7 \times 10^{-5} \, \text{mol} \, \text{dm}^{-3}$$

Then calculate pH from $[H^+(aq)]$

$$\therefore pH = -\log_{10}[H+(aq)]$$

$$= -\log_{10}(1.7 \times 10^{-5})$$

$\therefore$ pH of the buffer solution = 4.77

b First calculate $[H^+(aq)]$ using:

$$[H^+(aq)] = K_a \times \frac{[HA(aq)]}{[A^-(aq)]}$$

$$[H^+(aq)] = \frac{1.7 \times 10^{-5} \times 0.30}{0.10}$$

$$[H^+(aq)] = 5.1 \times 10^{-5} \, \text{mol} \, \text{dm}^{-3}$$

Then calculate pH from $[H^+(aq)]$

$$\therefore pH = -\log_{10}[H+(aq)]$$

$$= -\log_{10}(5.1 \times 10^{-5})$$

$\therefore$ pH of the buffer solution = 4.29

Control of pH in blood

Blood plasma in the human body has a normal pH of 7.4. If the pH falls below 7.0 or rises above 7.8 the results could be fatal. The buffer systems in the blood are extremely effective and protect the fluid from large changes in pH. Blood contains a number of buffering systems, the major one being the carbonic acid–hydrogen carbonate (bicarbonate) system:

$$H_2O(l) + CO_2(g) \; \rightleftharpoons \; H_2CO_3(aq) \; \rightleftharpoons \; HCO_3^-(aq) + H^+(aq)$$
$$\text{carbonic acid} \qquad \text{hydrogencarbonate}$$

Adding an acid to the system will increase the concentration of $H^+(aq)$, driving the equilibrium to the left-hand side. This increases the concentration of the carbonic acid, H_2CO_3, which in turn is decreased by an increased rate of breathing such that more $CO_2(g)$ is exhaled, resulting in the $H_2O(l) + CO_2(g) \rightleftharpoons H_2CO_3$ equilibrium moving further to the left to replace it. The two equilibria together resist the increase in acidity.

Adding an alkali to the system will decrease the concentration of $H^+(aq)$, driving the equilibrium to the right-hand side. This decreases the concentration of the carbonic acid, H_2CO_3, which in turn is increased by a decreased rate of breathing such that less $CO_2(g)$ is exhaled, resulting in the H_2CO_3 being replaced. The two equilibria together resist the increase in basicity.

Neutralisation

pH changes and indicators

Many **indicators** are weak acids and can be represented as HIn. The weak acid, HIn, and its conjugate base, In^-, have different colours. For example, for methyl orange:

An **indicator** is a substance that changes colour with a change in pH.

$$\underset{\text{weak acid}}{\underset{\text{red}}{HIn(aq)}} \rightleftharpoons H^+(aq) + \underset{\text{conjugate base}}{\underset{\text{yellow}}{In^-(aq)}}$$

At the end point of a titration HIn and In^- are present in equal concentrations.

Using methyl orange as indicator:

- at the end point [HIn] (red) = [In^-] (yellow)
- the colour at the end point is orange from equal proportions of red ([HIn]) and yellow ([In^-])
- the pH of the end point is called the pK_{In} of the indicator and $pK_{In} = -\log_{10}K_{In}$

pH ranges for common indicators

An indicator changes colour over a range of about two pH units, within which is the pK_{In} value of the indicator (Figure 16).

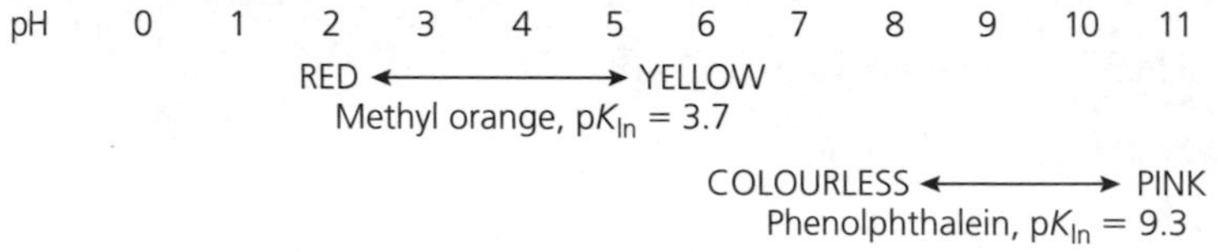

pH   0   1   2   3   4   5   6   7   8   9   10   11   12   13   14

RED ← → YELLOW
Methyl orange, $pK_{In} = 3.7$

COLOURLESS ← → PINK
Phenolphthalein, $pK_{In} = 9.3$

Figure 16

Choosing an indicator

When the acid and the base have completely reacted this is known as the **equivalence point**. At the equivalence point of the titration there is a sharp change in pH for a very small addition of acid or base.

The choice of a suitable indicator is best shown using titration curves.

Plotting titration curves

A titration curve shows the changes in pH during a titration.

Key features of titration curves

The pH changes rapidly at the near vertical portion of the titration curve. This is the **end point** of the titration.

The sharp change in pH is brought about by a very small addition of alkali, typically the addition of one drop.

The indicator is only suitable if its pK_{In} value is within the pH range of the near vertical portion of the titration curve.

Choosing an indicator using titration curves

On the titration curves in Figure 17:

- different combinations of strong and weak acids have been used
- the pK_{In} values are shown for the indicators methyl orange (MeO) and phenolphthalein (Ph)

Strong acid/strong alkali

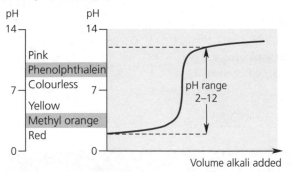

Methyl orange (**MeO**) ✓
Phenolphthalein (**Ph**) ✓

Strong acid/weak alkali

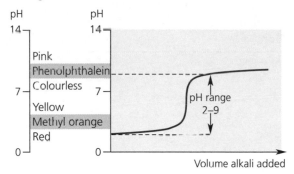

Methyl orange (**MeO**) ✓
Phenolphthalein (**Ph**) ✗

Weak acid/strong alkali

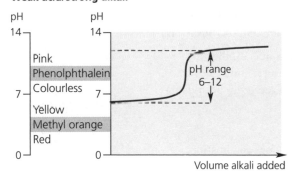

Methyl orange (**MeO**) ✗
Phenolphthalein (**Ph**) ✓

Weak acid/weak alkali

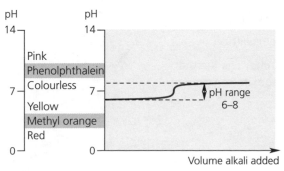

Methyl orange (**MeO**) ✗
Phenolphthalein (**Ph**) ✗

Figure 17

Measuring pH with a pH meter

A pH meter is a useful device that can be used to measure acidity. Before using a pH probe it has to be calibrated against buffer solutions of known pH. Once the pH meter has been calibrated the pH of a solution can be measured by placing the pH probe into the solution. Many meters also have a temperature setting because pH is temperature dependent.

A measurement of the pH of a known concentration of an acid or a base would indicate whether it was strong or weak.

Summary

Having revised **Rates, equilibrium and pH** you should now have an understanding of:
- orders of reaction and rate equations
- rate-determining step

- equilibrium, K_c and K_p
- acids, bases and conjugate pairs
- pK_a and pH
- buffers

■ Energy

Lattice enthalpy

Review of basic ideas on energetics

Chemical reactions are generally accompanied by a change in enthalpy (energy), usually in the form of heat energy. Reactions tend to be either exothermic or endothermic.

If the reaction mixture loses energy to its surroundings, the reaction is exothermic and ΔH is negative. If the reaction mixture gains energy from its surroundings, the reaction is endothermic and ΔH is positive. You should be able to represent both using energy profile diagrams.

You should also:
- understand and be able to define standard enthalpies of formation, combustion, reaction and neutralisation, as well as bond enthalpy
- be able to use Hess's law to determine unknown enthalpy changes

Lattice enthalpy and Born–Haber cycles

Lattice enthalpy indicates the strength of the ionic bonds in an ionic lattice.

The **lattice enthalpy** $(\Delta_{LE}H^{\ominus})$ of an ionic compound is the enthalpy change that accompanies the formation of 1 mol of an ionic compound from its constituent gaseous ions. For example:

$$Na^+(g) + Cl^-(g) \rightarrow Na^+Cl^-(s)$$

$\Delta_{LE}H^{\ominus}$ is exothermic.

It is almost impossible to measure lattice enthalpy experimentally, and so lattice enthalpy is calculated using a **Born–Haber** cycle. A Born–Haber cycle is similar to a Hess's cycle and enables the calculation of changes that cannot be measured directly by experiment.

The lattice enthalpy of sodium chloride can be calculated by considering the standard enthalpy of formation of NaCl(s). In order to form an ionic solid, both sodium and chlorine have to undergo a number of changes. These are outlined in Figure 18.

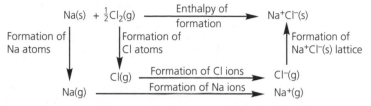

Figure 18

All of the changes in the cycle can be measured experimentally, except the formation of the Na^+Cl^-(s) lattice from its gaseous ions, that is, the lattice enthalpy. However, since all other steps in the cycle can be measured the lattice enthalpy can be calculated. This is done by adapting the above cycle and changing it into a Born–Haber cycle. The Born–Haber cycle is a combination of an enthalpy profile diagram and a Hess's cycle. The full Born–Haber cycle for sodium chloride is shown in Figure 19.

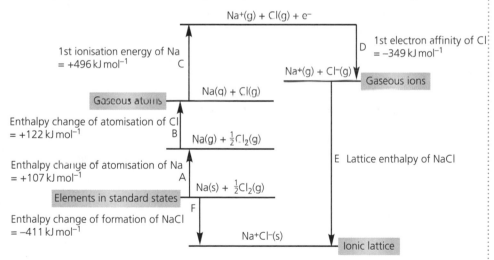

Figure 19

Using Hess's law:

A + B + C + D + E = F

$\Delta_{at}H^{\ominus}Na(g) + \Delta_{at}H^{\ominus}Cl(g) + \Delta_{IE}H^{\ominus}Na(g) + \Delta_{EA}H^{\ominus}Cl(g) + E = \Delta_fH^{\ominus}Na^+Cl^-(s)$

∴ +107 + 122 + 496 + (−349) + E = −411

Hence, the lattice energy E of Na^+Cl^-(s) = −787 kJ mol⁻¹.

Definitions for enthalpy changes

Formation of an ionic compound (step F in the Born–Haber cycle)

The **standard enthalpy change of formation** is usually exothermic for an ionic compound:

$$Na(s) + \tfrac{1}{2}Cl_2(g) \rightarrow Na^+Cl^-(s) \quad \Delta_f H^\ominus = -411\,\text{kJ}\,\text{mol}^{-1}$$

The **standard enthalpy change of formation**, $\Delta_f H^\ominus$, is the enthalpy change that takes place when 1 mol of a compound in its standard state is formed from its constituent elements in their standard states under standard conditions.

Formation of gaseous atoms (steps A and B in the Born–Haber cycle)

The **standard enthalpy change of atomisation** is always endothermic:

$$Na(s) \rightarrow Na(g) \qquad \Delta_{at} H^\ominus = +107\,\text{kJ}\,\text{mol}^{-1}$$

$$\tfrac{1}{2}Cl_2(g) \rightarrow Cl(g) \qquad \Delta_{at} H^\ominus = +122\,\text{kJ}\,\text{mol}^{-1}$$

For gaseous molecules this enthalpy change can be determined from the **bond dissociation enthalpy** — the enthalpy change required to break and separate one mole of bonds so that the resulting gaseous atoms exert no forces upon each other:

$$Cl\text{–}Cl(g) \rightarrow 2Cl(g) \qquad \Delta_{bde} H^\ominus = +244\,\text{kJ}\,\text{mol}^{-1}$$

$$\tfrac{1}{2}Cl\text{–}Cl(g) \rightarrow Cl(g) \qquad \Delta_{at} H^\ominus = +122\,\text{kJ}\,\text{mol}^{-1}$$

Formation of positive ions (step C in the Born–Haber cycle)

The **first ionisation energy** is always endothermic:

$$Na(g) \rightarrow Na^+(g) + e^- \quad \Delta_{IE} H^\ominus = +496\,\text{kJ}\,\text{mol}^{-1}$$

Formation of negative ions (step D in the Born–Haber cycle)

The **first electron affinity** is always exothermic:

$$Cl(g) + e^- \rightarrow Cl^-(g) \qquad \Delta_{EA} H^\ominus = -349\,\text{kJ}\,\text{mol}^{-1}$$

The **first electron affinity**, $\Delta_{EA} H^\ominus$, of an element is the enthalpy change that accompanies the addition of one electron to each atom in 1 mol of gaseous atoms to form 1 mol of gaseous 1$^-$ ions.

> **Exam tip**
>
> In most exams there is *at least* one question that asks for a definition; this can be worth as many as three marks. The difference between grade boundaries can sometimes be as low as six marks, so make sure you learn the definitions.

The **standard enthalpy change of atomisation**, $\Delta_{at} H^\ominus$, of an element is the enthalpy change that accompanies the formation of 1 mol of gaseous atoms from the element in its standard state.

The **first ionisation energy**, $\Delta_{IE} H^\ominus$, of an element is the enthalpy change that accompanies the removal of one electron from each atom in 1 mol of gaseous atoms to form 1 mol of gaseous 1$^+$ ions.

Formation of an ionic lattice (step E in the Born–Haber cycle)

$$Na^+(g) + Cl^-(g) \rightarrow Na^+Cl^-(s)$$

Exam tip

When constructing a Born–Haber cycle it is essential to show the change from *elements* to *gaseous atoms* to *gaseous ions* to *ionic lattice* (Figure 20).

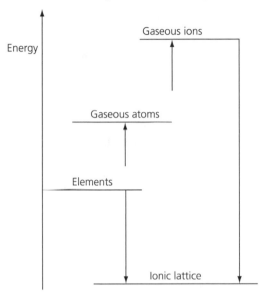

Figure 20

Calculation of lattice enthalpy

The lattice enthalpy for magnesium chloride and for magnesium oxide can be calculated using the data in Table 4.

Table 4

Stage	Standard enthalpy change	Equation	$\Delta H/\text{kJ}\,\text{mol}^{-1}$
A	Formation of $MgCl_2(s)$	$Mg(s) + Cl_2(g) \rightarrow MgCl_2(s)$	−641
B	Formation of $MgO(s)$	$Mg(s) + \frac{1}{2}O_2(g) \rightarrow MgO(s)$	−602
C	Atomisation of magnesium	$Mg(s) \rightarrow Mg(g)$	+148
D	Atomisation of chlorine	$\frac{1}{2}Cl_2(g) \rightarrow Cl(g)$	+122
E	Atomisation of oxygen	$\frac{1}{2}O_2(g) \rightarrow O(g)$	+249
F	First ionisation energy of Mg	$Mg(g) \rightarrow Mg^+(g) + 1e^-$	+738
G	Second ionisation energy of Mg	$Mg^+(g) \rightarrow Mg^{2+}(g) + 1e^-$	+1451
H	First electron affinity of Cl	$Cl(g) + 1e^- \rightarrow Cl^-(g)$	−349
I	First electron affinity of O	$O(g) + 1e^- \rightarrow O^-(g)$	−141
J	Second electron affinity of O	$O^-(g) + 1e^- \rightarrow O^{2-}(g)$	+798

The Born–Haber cycle for magnesium chloride is shown in Figure 21.

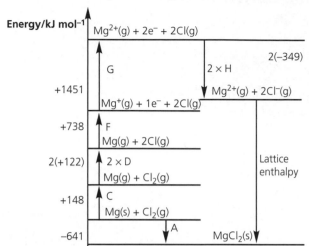

Figure 21

Applying Hess's law to the Born–Haber cycle gives:

$$A = C + 2D + F + G + 2H + LE$$

so,

$$LE = A - C - 2D - F - G - 2H$$

The lattice enthalpy of magnesium chloride is:

$$= -641 - 148 - 244 - 738 - 1451 - (-698)$$

$$= -2524 \, kJ \, mol^{-1}$$

The Born–Haber cycle for magnesium oxide (Figure 22) is similar but in order to form the oxide ion, O^{2-} the oxygen atom needs to gain two electrons and consequently has two electron affinities. The first electron affinity is exothermic but the second electron affinity is endothermic.

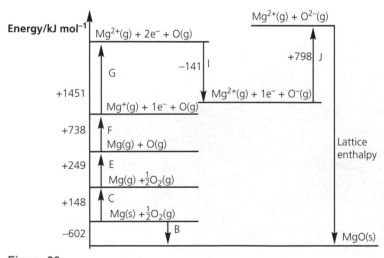

Figure 22

> ### Exam tip
>
> When constructing a Born–Haber cycle for $MgCl_2$ students often lose marks by forgetting to double the value for the atomisation energy and the electron affinity of Cl.

The lattice enthalpy of MgO(s) can be shown, by calculation, to be $-3\,845\,\text{kJ}\,\text{mol}^{-1}$.

Factors affecting the size of lattice enthalpies

The strength of an ionic lattice and the value of its lattice enthalpy depend upon ionic radius and ionic charge.

Effect of ionic size

The effect of ionic size is demonstrated by the examples in Table 5.

Table 5

Compound	Lattice enthalpy/ kJ mol⁻¹	Ions	Effect of ionic radius of halide ion
NaCl	−787		Ionic radius increases, charge remains the same, hence charge density decreases
NaBr	−751		Attraction between ions decreases, hence lattice energy becomes less negative
NaI	−705		

Note that lattice energy has a negative value and you should use the term 'becomes less/more negative' instead of 'becomes bigger/smaller' to describe lattice enthalpies.

Effect of ionic charge

The strongest ionic lattices contain **small, highly charged ions** (see Table 6).

Table 6

Na⁺	Mg²⁺	Al³⁺	P³⁻	S²⁻	Cl⁻

Charge increases and produces *more* attraction *and* ionic radius decreases and produces *more* attraction	Charge increases and produces *more* attraction *but* ionic radius increases and produces *less* attraction, *however*, the increase in the charge from −1 to −3 outweighs the slight increase in radii, and so attraction increases

Knowledge check 25

Write equations to illustrate:

a atomisation energy of Cl_2

b lattice enthalpy of $CaCl_2$

c second ionisation energy of Mg

Exam tip

If asked to predict the size of lattice enthalpy it is best to avoid using terms like *bigger* or *smaller*. Lattice enthalpy is always negative and it is best to use terms such as *more negative* or *less negative*.

Knowledge check 26

Arrange the following in order of size of lattice enthalpy, with the most negative first:

a $NaBr$, KBr, $MgBr_2$

b $CaCl_2$, $BaCl_2$, CaF_2, $BaBr_2$

Enthalpy change of hydration

Solubility and enthalpies of hydration

The concept of a Born–Haber cycle can be extended to provide a partial explanation for the solubility of substances in water. To understand this, another new enthalpy term needs to be introduced. This is the enthalpy of hydration of an ion, which is defined as the enthalpy change that occurs when 1 mol of gaseous ions is completely hydrated by water.

It is therefore the enthalpy change for the process:

$$X^{n+}(g) \rightarrow X^{n+}(aq)$$

The standard **enthalpy of hydration** is quoted under the usual conditions of 25°C and 101 kPa.

In the case of hydration the attraction is either between a cation and the oxygen atom of a water molecule or between an anion and a hydrogen atom of the water molecule (Figure 23). This occurs because of the dipoles present in water, which you should be familiar with from year 1 of the A-level course.

> The **enthalpy of hydration** of an ion, $\Delta_{hyd}H^{\ominus}$, is defined as the enthalpy change that occurs when 1 mol of gaseous ions are completely hydrated by water.

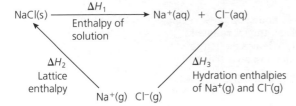

Figure 23

Like lattice enthalpy, the enthalpy change of hydration also depends on the ionic radius and the size of the charge of the ion. As with lattice enthalpy, the greater the charge density the greater the attraction.

Values of lattice enthalpies and enthalpies of hydration relate to the **enthalpy of solution**, which is the enthalpy change that occurs when an ionic solid dissolves in water. A typical enthalpy cycle for sodium chloride is shown in Figure 24.

> The **enthalpy of solution** of a compound, $\Delta_{sol}H^{\ominus}$, is defined as the enthalpy change when 1 mol of that compound dissolves completely in excess water.

```
NaCl(s) ———————ΔH₁————————→ Na⁺(aq)  +  Cl⁻(aq)
                Enthalpy of
                solution

     ΔH₂                        ΔH₃
    Lattice                  Hydration enthalpies
   enthalpy                  of Na⁺(g) and Cl⁻(g)
            Na⁺(g)  Cl⁻(g)
```

Figure 24

Applying Hess's law, $\Delta H_2 + \Delta H_1 = \Delta H_3$, such that $\Delta H_1 = \Delta H_3 - \Delta H_2$, where:

- ΔH_1 = enthalpy of solution
- ΔH_2 = lattice enthalpy of $NaCl(s)$ = $-781\,kJ\,mol^{-1}$
- ΔH_3 = enthalpy of hydration of the Na^+ ion (-418) + enthalpy of hydration of the Cl^- ion (-338) = $-756\,kJ\,mol^{-1}$

$$\Delta H_1 = \Delta H_3 - \Delta H_2 = -756 + 781 = +25\,kJ\,mol^{-1}$$

It might seem odd that the dissolving of sodium chloride is endothermic and yet sodium chloride readily dissolves in water at 25°C. This suggests that there is some other factor that is encouraging the dissolving to take place. It is an energy term called **entropy** and this is discussed in the next section.

Exam tip

This could be tested by providing you with a Born–Haber diagram and asking you to deduce the value of any one step. The Born–Haber diagram for NaCl is shown in Figure 25.

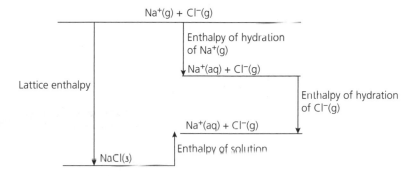

Figure 25

Knowledge check 27

Write equations to illustrate the following:

a the enthalpy of hydration of calcium ions

b the enthalpy of solution of $Ca(OH)_2(s)$

c the lattice enthalpy of $Ca(OH)_2(s)$

Entropy

Hess's law and the use of the Born–Haber cycle allow important information to be obtained concerning enthalpy changes that occur as a result of chemical reactions. But knowledge of enthalpy changes alone is insufficient to provide a certain answer as to whether a reaction will take place or not. Further information is needed about another energy change that takes place during a reaction. The information required is known as entropy.

When a reaction occurs enthalpy is either absorbed (endothermic) or released (exothermic) in the form of heat. In addition some energy is either absorbed or released as a result of the re-distribution of the particles when the products are formed. The extent of this energy depends largely on the physical state of the substances and on the temperature. Entropy is the term used to measure this quantity of energy and it is given the symbol S. We will be concerned in this course only with the reaction itself (known as the reaction system) although a more detailed study would include the effect on the surroundings.

Solids are more ordered than liquids, while gases are the least ordered. It follows that the most energy/entropy is required to hold a solid in its ordered state. The particles of a gas are less restrained than in a liquid and energy/entropy is not used up in restricting their freedom of movement.

The enthalpy change for the melting of ice to water at 0°C is:

$$H_2O(s) \rightarrow H_2O(l) \qquad \Delta H = +6.02\,kJ\,mol^{-1}$$

The reaction therefore does not look possible, but we all know that ice does melt at 0°C. This can be explained because the change in entropy, as melting occurs, releases sufficient energy to counteract the positive enthalpy. The energy required to hold the rigid structure of the ice in place is released as the less restrained molecules of water are produced.

Enthalpy and entropy have a number of important differences, as outlined in Table 7.

Table 7

Enthalpy	Entropy
If enthalpy is released when a reaction occurs ΔH is negative	If entropy is released when a reaction occurs ΔS is positive
The energy unit is usually in $kJ\,mol^{-1}$	The energy unit is usually in $J\,mol^{-1}\,K^{-1}$

Entropy always increases (ΔS is positive) when there is a greater opportunity for energy to be spread out as a result of a change. It follows that entropy increases when any of the following occur.

- A solid become becomes a liquid. Entropy is released and ΔS is positive — more disordered.
- A liquid becomes a gas. Entropy is released and ΔS is positive — more disordered.
- A solid dissolves in a liquid to form a solution. Entropy is released and ΔS is positive — more disordered.
- A reaction results in products with a greater degree of freedom of movement. For example, this could be because a gas is produced when a solid reacts, for example, $CaCO_3(s) \rightarrow CaO(s) + CO_2(g)$. Entropy is released and ΔS is positive — more disordered.
- When a reaction produces more particles in the same state, for example, $C_3H_8(g) + 5O_2(g) \rightarrow 3CO_2(g) + 4H_2O(g)$. Entropy is released and ΔS is positive — more disordered.
- The temperature rises, even if there is no change in state. Entropy is released and ΔS is positive — more disordered.

Calculating entropy changes

Calculations to determine ΔS are similar to calculations for ΔH, although it must be remembered that if ΔS is positive, it means the process releases entropy.

The change in entropy can be calculated using:

$$\Delta S = \Sigma(\text{entropy of products}) - \Sigma(\text{entropy of reactants})$$

Exam tip

You will not be asked to explain what 'entropy' is. It is a difficult concept and even experts disagree. You may be asked to predict whether or not entropy increases in a reaction, in which case simply use the state symbols as a guide. Compare the number of moles of gas or liquid or solid on each side of the equation.

Knowledge check 28

For each of the following reactions predict whether the reaction will have a positive or negative value for the entropy change:
a $H_2O(g) \rightarrow H_2O(s)$
b $NaOH(s) \rightarrow NaOH(aq)$
c $2Mg(s) + O_2(g) \rightarrow 2MgO(s)$
d $2SO_2(g) + O_2(g) \rightarrow 2SO_3(g)$

Example

Calculate the entropy change for the reaction $3O_2(g) \rightarrow 2O_3(g)$ under standard conditions, given that $S^\ominus$ for O_3 is $238.8\,J\,mol^{-1}\,K^{-1}$, and $S^\ominus$ for O_2 is $205\,J\,mol^{-1}\,K^{-1}$.

Answer

$\Delta S = \Sigma(\text{entropy of products}) - \Sigma(\text{entropy of reactants})$

$\Delta S = 2 \times (238.8) \qquad - 3 \times (205)$

$\quad = -137.4\,J\,mol^{-1}\,K^{-1}$

You should be able to anticipate the sign of ΔS by the fact that 3 mol of O_2 gas have changed to 2 mol of O_3 gas. When a reaction produces fewer particles in the same state, ΔS is negative.

Knowledge check 29

Calculate the entropy change when sodium reacts with oxygen.

$S^\ominus$ (sodium) $= 51.0\,J\,mol^{-1}\,K^{-1}$;

$S^\ominus$ (oxygen) $= 102.5\,J\,mol^{-1}\,K^{-1}$;

$S^\ominus$ (sodium oxide) $= 72.8\,J\,mol^{-1}\,K^{-1}$

Free energy

The change in the entropy of a reaction can be combined with the change in enthalpy to provide an answer to the question as to whether a chemical reaction is feasible.

A new term must be introduced called the free energy (strictly this is known as the Gibbs free energy), which is given the symbol G. The free energy change of a reaction relates to the enthalpy and entropy changes by the Gibbs' equation:

$\Delta G = \Delta H - T\Delta S$

ΔG provides a certain answer as to whether a given reaction will be feasible. If ΔG is negative, the reaction will definitely be feasible and if ΔG is positive then, at least at the particular temperature chosen, the reaction will not be feasible.

Any reaction will fit one of four possible scenarios:

- **ΔH is negative and ΔS is positive**. The reaction will always be feasible.
- **ΔH is positive and ΔS is negative**. The reaction will never be feasible.
- **ΔH is negative and ΔS is negative**. ΔH favours the reaction, but $T\Delta S$ resists the change. The reaction will be feasible when $\Delta H > T\Delta S$ and is therefore more likely to be feasible at low temperatures.
- **ΔH is positive and ΔS is positive**. ΔH resists the reaction but $T\Delta S$ favours the change. The reaction will be feasible when $\Delta H < T\Delta S$ and is therefore more likely to be feasible at high temperatures.

If $\Delta G = 0$, then the system will be at the point of being feasible and $\Delta H = T\Delta S$. The enthalpy change for the melting of ice to water at 0°C is $H_2O(s) \rightarrow H_2O(l)$ $\Delta H = +6.02\,kJ\,mol^{-1}$. At 0°C (273 K) $\Delta G = 0$ such that $\Delta S = \Delta H/T$, hence the entropy change when ice melts is:

$$\Delta S = \frac{\Delta H}{T} = \frac{6.02\,kJ\,mol^{-1}}{273\,K}$$

but entropy is measured in $J\,mol^{-1}\,K^{-1}$, so:

$$\frac{6020\,J\,mol^{-1}}{273\,K} = 22.0\,J\,mol^{-1}\,K^{-1}$$

For a chemical reaction, the values of ΔH and ΔS must be calculated and then the value of the temperature, T, for which ΔG is zero can be established. It should first be noted, however, that equilibrium can never be reached for a reaction for which either ΔH is negative and ΔS is positive (because the reaction is always feasible) or ΔH is positive and ΔS is negative (because the reaction is never feasible), but where ΔH and ΔS have the same sign it will be possible to find the equilibrium temperature, noting that as $\Delta G = 0$, $\Delta H = T\Delta S$, so:

$$T = \frac{\Delta H}{\Delta S}$$

Calculating free energy changes

If tables of information are provided, then calculating the value of ΔG for a reaction is identical to the process of calculating ΔH.

If values for ΔH and S are available for each component in the equation then it is a little more laborious but ΔG can be calculated for each substance in turn and then the overall ΔG for the reaction can be determined.

Example

Use the data below to calculate the temperature at which the reaction $2NO(g) + O_2(g) \rightarrow 2NO_2(g)$ reaches equilibrium.

	$\Delta_f H^\ominus / kJ\,mol^{-1}$	$S^\ominus / J\,mol^{-1}\,K^{-1}$
NO(g)	90.4	210.5
O$_2$(g)	0	204.9
NO$_2$(g)	33.2	240.0

Answer

Use:

- $\Delta H = \Sigma(\text{enthalpy of products}) - \Sigma(\text{enthalpy of reactants})$
- $\Delta S = \Sigma(\text{entropy of products}) - \Sigma(\text{entropy of reactants})$
- at equilibrium, $\Delta G = 0$, so $T = \Delta H/\Delta S$

ΔH for the reaction is:

$$(2 \times 33.2) - (2 \times 90.4) = -114.4\,kJ\,mol^{-1}$$

and

$$\Delta S = (2 \times 240.0) - [(2 \times 210.5) + 204.9] = -145.9\,J\,mol^{-1}\,K^{-1}$$

Therefore (remembering to convert ΔS from J into kJ):

$$T = \frac{-114.4}{-0.1459} = 784\,K \text{ or } 511°C$$

Exam tip

When using $\Delta G = \Delta H - T\Delta S$ you must remember that the units of ΔG and ΔH are both $kJ\,mol^{-1}$ *but* ΔS is measured in $J\,mol^{-1}\,K^{-1}$. Therefore ΔS has to be converted into $kJ\,mol^{-1}\,K^{-1}$.

Redox and electrode potentials

Ionic equations

To write ionic equations correctly, it is essential to remember the following points.

- Ionic substances that are solid do not have free-moving ions and therefore their ions cannot react independently of each other. In an ionic equation their complete formula must be given.
- Compounds of metals and strong acids in aqueous solution will always be split into their ions. These ions can, and do, react independently of each other.
- Covalent compounds exist as complete molecules and are always shown as complete entities in the ionic equation.
- It is important to include the state symbols in all ionic equations.
- It is essential to balance both symbols and charge.

Redox and oxidation numbers

The displacement reaction between chlorine and bromide (Figure 26) is an example of a redox reaction that you met in Module 3:

$$Cl_2(g) + 2Br^-(aq) \rightarrow 2Cl^-(aq) + Br_2(aq)$$

Remember that **o**xidation **i**s **l**oss, **r**eduction **i**s **g**ain ('OILRIG').

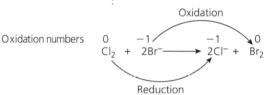

Figure 26

Oxidation number

Oxidation number is a convenient way of quickly identifying whether or not a substance has undergone either oxidation or reduction. To work out the oxidation number you must first learn the few simple rules shown in Table 8.

Table 8

Rule	Example
1	All elements in their natural state have oxidation number = 0 H_2, oxidation number of H = 0
2	The oxidation numbers of any molecule always add up to zero H_2O, sum of oxidation numbers = 0
3	The oxidation numbers of any ion always add up to the charge of the ion. SO_4^{2-}, sum of oxidation numbers = –2
When calculating the oxidation numbers of elements in either a molecule or an ion you should apply the following order of priority.	
(i)	Groups 1, 2 and 3 elements are always +1, +2 and +3, respectively
(ii)	Fluorine is always –1
(iii)	Hydrogen is usually +1
(iv)	Oxygen is usually –2
(v)	Chlorine is usually –1

Content Guidance

If you make sure that you apply these rules rigidly in the sequence indicated it should be relatively simple to deduce any oxidation number.

Consider the reaction of zinc and aqueous copper sulfate:

$$Zn(s) + CuSO_4(aq) \rightarrow ZnSO_4(aq) + Cu(s)$$

It is often helpful to immediately write the oxidation numbers above each element in the equation:

Oxidation numbers

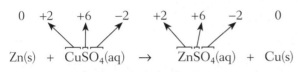

In any redox reaction the oxidation number of one element increases while the oxidation number of a second element decreases. Zn increases from 0 to +2, while Cu decreases from +2 to 0, such that the ionic equation can be written as:

$$Zn(s) + Cu^{2+}(aq) \rightarrow Zn^{2+}(aq) + Cu(s)$$

The Zn is oxidised, losing two electrons and becoming a Zn^{2+} ion. The electrons are taken up by the Cu^{2+} ion as it is reduced to Cu metal. It is possible to write ionic half-equations:

$$Zn(s) \rightarrow Zn^{2+}(aq) + 2e^- \qquad \text{Oxidation (loss of electrons)}$$

$$Cu^{2+}(aq) + 2e^- \rightarrow Cu(s) \qquad \text{Reduction (gain of electrons)}$$

It follows that the $Cu^{2+}(aq)$ is the **oxidising agent** and the $Zn(s)$ is the **reducing agent**.

It should also be possible to use ionic half-equations to construct a full ionic equation. When Cu(s) is added to aqueous $AgNO_3(aq)$, $Cu^{2+}(aq)$ and Ag(s) are formed. The ionic half-equations are:

$$Cu(s) \rightarrow Cu^{2+}(aq) + 2e^- \qquad \text{Oxidation (loss of electrons)}$$

$$Ag^+(aq) + e^- \rightarrow Ag(s) \qquad \text{Reduction (gain of electrons)}$$

In any two ionic half-equations the number of electrons released (by oxidation) must be the same as the number required for the reduction. Cu(s) supplies two electrons as it oxidises to $Cu^{2+}(aq)$ but each $Ag^+(aq)$ requires only one electron to be reduced to Ag(s). Therefore it will be necessary to use two $Ag^+(aq)$ for every one Cu(s), such that:

$$Cu(s) \rightarrow Cu^{2+}(aq) + 2e^-$$

$$2Ag^+(aq) + 2e^- \rightarrow 2Ag(s)$$

The overall equation is then obtained by adding the two half-equations together, but excluding the electrons:

$$2Ag^+(aq) + Cu(s) \rightarrow 2Ag(s) + Cu^{2+}(aq)$$

Oxidising agents are chemicals that can oxidise other atoms, molecules or ions, by taking electrons away from them.

Reducing agents are chemicals that can reduce other atoms, molecules or ions by giving electrons to them.

Use each of the following pairs of half-equations to construct an overall equation for the reaction. You *must* balance each half-equation before constructing the overall equation.

a $MnO_4^-(aq) + H^+(aq) \rightarrow Mn^{2+}(aq) + H_2O(l)$ $V^{2+}(aq) \rightarrow V^{3+}(aq)$
b $MnO_4^-(aq) + H^+(aq) \rightarrow Mn^{2+}(aq) + H_2O(l)$ $V^{2+}(aq) + H_2O \rightarrow VO_3^-(aq) + H^+(aq)$
c $Cr_2O_7^{2-}(aq) + H^+(aq) \rightarrow Cr^{3+}(aq) + H_2O(l)$ $SO_2(aq) + H_2O(l) \rightarrow SO_4^{2-}(aq) + H^+(aq)$
d $NO_3^-(aq) \rightarrow NO(g)$ $Cu(s) \rightarrow Cu^{2+}(aq)$

Electrode potentials

The **standard electrode potentials** of two half-cells can be combined to give a **standard cell potential**. This is important and it defines whether or not a reaction is feasible.

The standard hydrogen electrode is shown in Figure 27.

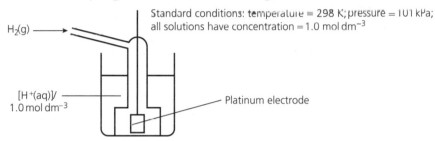

Standard conditions: temperature = 298 K; pressure = 101 kPa; all solutions have concentration = 1.0 mol dm^{-3}

$H_2(g)$

$[H^+(aq)]/$
1.0 mol dm^{-3}

Platinum electrode

Figure 27

To provide a better surface for the hydrogen, the platinum electrode is usually coated with very finely divided platinum known as platinum black. This cell is connected via an external circuit and through a salt bridge to the other cell. The voltage measured then gives what is known as the electrode potential of the cell, on a scale with the half-reaction $2H^+(aq) + 2e^- \rightarrow H_2(g)$ being given the arbitrary value of zero.

Measure the standard electrode potentials

For metals the system shown in Figure 28 applies.

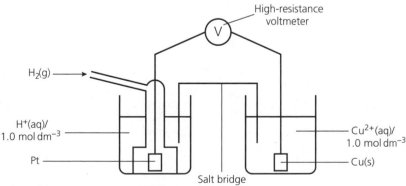

High-resistance voltmeter

V

$H_2(g)$

$H^+(aq)/$
1.0 mol dm^{-3}

Pt

Salt bridge

$Cu^{2+}(aq)/$
1.0 mol dm^{-3}

$Cu(s)$

Standard conditions: temperature = 298 K; pressure = 101 kPa;
all solutions have concentration = 1.0 mol dm^{-3}

Figure 28

When you have balanced an equation *always* double-check to make sure that the total charge on each side of the equation balances, as well as the symbols.

The **standard electrode potential** is the potential difference (the difference in voltage) between one half-cell (for example, a metal in contact with its metal ions) and the standard hydrogen electrode when measured under standard conditions ($T = 298K$, $P = 101$ kPa and concentration = 1.0 mol dm^{-3}).

The **standard cell potential** is the voltage formed when two half-cells are connected and the voltage is measured using a voltmeter of very high resistance, under standard conditions ($T = 298K$, $P = 101$ kPa and concentration = 1.0 mol dm^{-3}).

For non-metals/ions of the same element in different oxidation states the system in Figure 29 applies.

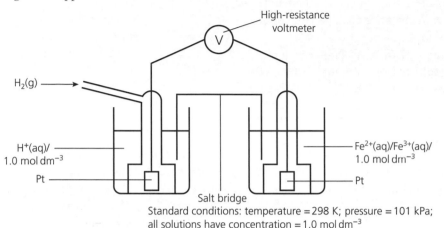

Figure 29

The salt bridge is made of a porous material soaked in a saturated solution of KNO_3. The salt bridge completes the circuit without mixing the solutions by allowing the passage of ions.

Some common cell potentials are listed in Table 9.

Table 9

Half-cell	$E^{\ominus}$/V	Half-cell	$E^{\ominus}$/V
$F_2(g) + 2e^- \rightleftharpoons 2F^-(aq)$	+2.87	$Fe^{3+}(aq) + e^- \rightleftharpoons Fe^{2+}(aq)$	+0.77
$MnO_4^-(aq) + 8H^+(aq) + 5e^- \rightleftharpoons Mn^{2+}(aq) + 4H_2O(l)$	+1.52	$Cu^{2+}(aq) + 2e^- \rightleftharpoons Cu(s)$	+0.34
$Cl_2(g) + 2e^- \rightleftharpoons 2Cl^-(aq)$	+1.36	**$2H^+(aq) + 2e^- \rightleftharpoons H_2(g)$**	**0.00**
$Cr_2O_7^{2-}(aq) + 14H^+(aq) + 6e^- \rightleftharpoons 2Cr^{3+}(aq) + 7H_2O(l)$	+1.33	$Zn^{2+}(aq) + 2e^- \rightleftharpoons Zn(s)$	−0.76
$Ag^+(aq) + e^- \rightleftharpoons Ag(s)$	+0.80	$K^+(aq) + e^- \rightleftharpoons K(s)$	−2.92

Half-cells with positive $E^{\ominus}$ favour the forward reaction and gain electrons. Those with a negative $E^{\ominus}$ favour the reverse reaction and lose electrons. $F_2(g)$ has the highest $+E^{\ominus}$ and readily gains electrons to form $F^-(aq)$ ions. F_2 is a powerful oxidising agent. By contrast, $K(s)$ readily loses an electron to form $K^+(aq)$ and is a powerful reducing agent.

The standard electrode cell can be calculated by using any two half-cells. The $E^{\ominus}$ values for the zinc and copper systems are:

$Zn^{2+}(aq) + 2e^- \rightleftharpoons Zn(s)$ $\qquad$ −0.76 V

$Cu^{2+}(aq) + 2e^- \rightleftharpoons Cu(s)$ $\qquad$ +0.34 V

The values indicate that the $Cu^{2+}(aq)$ moves in the forward reaction while the $Zn(s)$ favours the reverse reaction. Each half-cell can now be re-written as:

$Cu^{2+}(aq) + 2e^- \rightarrow Cu(s)$ $\qquad$ +0.34 V

$Zn(s) \rightarrow Zn^{2+}(aq) + 2e^-$ $\qquad$ +0.76 V

Cell potential $\qquad$ +1.10 V

Exam tip

Each of Fe^{2+} (aq) and Fe^{3+} (aq) must have concentration $1.0\,mol\,dm^{-3}$ or , if it is not possible to form a $1.0\,mol\,dm^{-3}$ solution then each solution must be of the same concentration (equimolar).

Example

Acidified $H^+(aq)/MnO_4^-(aq)$ is a good oxidising agent and can be used to prepare $Cl_2(g)$ by the oxidation of $Cl^-(aq)$ ions. Calculate the cell potential and deduce the balanced equation.

$$MnO_4^-(aq) + 8H^+(aq) + 5e^- \rightleftharpoons Mn^{2+} + 4H_2O(l) \qquad +1.52\,V$$

$$Cl_2(g) + 2e^- \rightleftharpoons 2Cl^-(aq) \qquad +1.36\,V$$

Answer

Both electrode potentials are positive but $H^+(aq)/MnO_4^-(aq)$ is most positive and therefore more likely to move to the right, such that:

$$MnO_4^-(aq) + 8H^+(aq) + 5e^- \rightarrow Mn^{2+} + 4H_2O(l) \qquad +1.52\,V$$

$$2Cl^-(aq) \rightarrow Cl_2(g) + 2e^- \qquad -1.36\,V$$

Cell potential $\qquad +0.16\,V$

Both half-equations must have the same number of electrons. MnO_4^- is multiplied by 2 to give $10e^-$ and Cl^- is multiplied by 5.

$$2MnO_4^-(aq) + 16H^+(aq) + 10e^- \rightarrow 2Mn^{2+} + 8H_2O(l)$$

$$10Cl^- \rightarrow 5Cl_2(g) + 10e^-$$

$$2MnO_4^-(aq) + 16H^+(aq) + 10Cl^- \rightarrow 2Mn^{2+} + 8H_2O(l) + 5Cl_2(g)$$

Net charge on left side is   Net charge on right side is +4
$(-2 + 16 - 10) = +4$

> **Exam tip**
>
> Always double check to ensure that the charges on both sides of the full ionic equation balance.

Knowledge check 31

Use the standard electrode potentials in the table to calculate the cell potential for each of the pairs of half-cells:

	$E^\ominus$		$E^\ominus$
$Mg^{2+}(aq) + 2e- \rightleftharpoons Mg(s)$	$-2.37\,V$	$Zn^{2+}(aq) + 2e^- \rightleftharpoons Zn(s)$	$-0.76\,V$
$Sn^{4+}(aq) + 2e^- \rightleftharpoons Sn^{2+}(aq)$	$+0.15\,V$	$I_2(aq) + 2e^- \rightleftharpoons 2I^-(aq)$	$+0.54\,V$
$Fe^{3+}(aq) + e^- \rightleftharpoons Fe^{2+}(aq)$	$+0.77\,V$	$Br_2(aq) + 2e^- \rightleftharpoons 2Br^-(aq)$	$+1.09\,V$

a $Mg(s)/Mg^{2+}(aq)$ and $Zn(s)/Zn^{2+}(aq)$
b $Sn^{4+}(aq)/Sn^{2+}(aq)$ and $Fe^{3+}(aq)/Fe^{2+}(aq)$
c $I_2(aq)/2I^-(aq)$ and $Br_2(aq)/2Br^-(aq)$
d $Zn(s)/Zn^{2+}(aq)$ and $I_2(aq)/2I^-(aq)$
e $Sn^{4+}(aq)/Sn^{2+}(aq)$ and $Br_2(aq)/2Br^-(aq)$

Effect of concentration on the feasibility of reactions

A positive cell potential indicates that a reaction is feasible but it gives no indication as to how fast a reaction will occur. The cell potential of the reaction between $H^+(aq)$/$MnO_4^-(aq)$ and Cl^- is only $+0.16\,V$ but the reaction takes place quickly despite the low overall potential.

Cell potentials are calculated assuming standard conditions, and if the concentration of one component in a half-cell is changed, according to le Chatelier's principle the equilibrium will shift in such a way as to minimise the effect of the change.

If, for example, the equilibrium $Fe^{3+}(aq) + e^- \rightleftharpoons Fe^{2+}(aq)$, for which $E^\ominus = +0.77\,V$, is carried out with a reduced concentration of $Fe^{2+}(aq)$, then this will encourage a movement from left to right in the equilibrium, which will then cause the value of the electrode potential to increase. If there is a reduced concentration of $Fe^{3+}(aq)$ then the equilibrium will move to the left and the value of $E^\ominus$ will decrease. In both cases, a very large change would be required to make any noticeable difference. As a general rule of thumb, a ten-fold change in concentration only changes the electrode potential of a half-reaction by $0.06\,V$ or less.

Storage cells and fuel cells

Storage cells

Storage cells are commonly referred to as batteries and are used in appliances to supply electricity. Electrode potential can be used to predict the possible voltage of a battery but there is no need to remember the details or constructions of any particular cell. You will not be asked in any exam to recall any particular type of cell but you may be expected to interpret data that have been provided.

> **Knowledge check 32**
>
> NiCd cells are used in rechargeable storage cells (batteries). The electrolyte in a NiCd cell is KOH(aq). The standard electrode potentials for the redox systems in a NiCd cell are:
>
> $NiO(OH) + H_2O + e^- \rightleftharpoons Ni(OH)_2 + OH^- \qquad E^\ominus = +0.45\,V$
>
> $Cd(OH)_2 + 2e^- \rightleftharpoons Cd + 2OH^- \qquad E^\ominus = -0.80\,V$
>
> **a** What is the standard cell potential of a NiCd cell?
> **b** What is the overall cell reaction of a NiCd cell?
> **c** Suggest how the battery could be recharged.

Fuel cells

Fuel cells can produce electrical power from the chemical reaction of a fuel (such as hydrogen, hydrocarbons or alcohols) with oxygen. The fuel cell operates like a conventional storage cell except that the fuels are supplied as gases externally. The cell will therefore operate more or less indefinitely so long as the supply is maintained.

The hydrogen–oxygen fuel cell is used widely and illustrates the general principles behind fuel cells. The electrolyte is an acid or alkaline membrane that allows ions to move from one compartment of the cell to the other. (In other words, it acts like a salt bridge.)

In alkaline solution, hydrogen reacts with hydroxide ions at the negative electrode to form water while, at the positive electrode, oxygen reacts with water to form hydroxide ions:

$$H_2(g) + 2OH^-(aq) \rightarrow 2H_2O(l) + 2e^- \qquad E^\ominus = +0.83\,V$$

$$\tfrac{1}{2}O_2(g) + H_2O(l) + 2e^- \rightarrow 2OH^-(aq) \qquad E^\ominus = +0.40\,V$$

In an acidic solution, hydrogen is converted to hydrogen ions at the negative electrode while, at the positive electrode, oxygen reacts with hydrogen ions to make water:

$$H_2(g) \rightarrow 2H^+(aq) + 2e^- \qquad E^\ominus = 0.00\,V$$

$$\tfrac{1}{2}O_2(g) + 2H^+(aq) + 2e^- \rightarrow H_2O(l) \qquad E^\ominus = +1.23\,V$$

The overall reaction in both cases is the same and is equivalent to the burning of the fuel:

$$H_2(g) + \tfrac{1}{2}O_2(g) \rightarrow 2H_2O(l) \qquad E^\ominus = +1.23\,V$$

Other fuel cells can be constructed using different 'fuels'. For example, a methanol fuel cell uses methanol instead of hydrogen. The overall reaction that is occurring within the cell is again equivalent to burning the methanol, so that the overall equation is:

$$CH_3OH + 1\tfrac{1}{2}O_2 \rightarrow CO_2 + 2H_2O$$

The processes that take place at the electrodes mirror this equation. In an acidic medium:

- at the positive electrode

$$1\tfrac{1}{2}O_2 + 6H^+ + 6e^- \rightarrow 3H_2O$$

- at the negative electrode

$$CH_3OH + H_2O \rightarrow CO_2 + 6H^+ + 6e^-$$

By combining these two equations it gives:

$$1\tfrac{1}{2}O_2 + 6H^+ + CH_3OH + H_2O \rightarrow 3H_2O + CO_2 + 6H^+$$

which simplifies to:

$$CH_3OH + 1\tfrac{1}{2}O_2 \rightarrow CO_2 + 2H_2O$$

which is the equation for the combustion of methanol.

Exam tip

Fuels other than hydrogen can also be used in fuel cells. In any fuel cell the electrons always flow (via the external circuit) *from* the electrode to which the fuel is supplied.

Knowledge check 33

Ethanol, C_2H_5OH, can be used as the fuel in a fuel cell. Construct equations for the overall reaction and for the reactions at each electrode. Assume that an acidic electrolyte is used.

Summary

Having revised **Energy** you should now have an understanding of:
- lattice enthalpy and Born–Haber cycles
- enthalpies of solution and hydration
- entropy, and the relationship between free energy, enthalpy and entropy
- electrode potentials
- storage cells and fuel cells

Transition elements

Properties

The fourth period runs from K to Kr:

s-block		d-block										p-block					
K	Ca	Sc	Ti	V	Cr	Mn	Fe	Co	Ni	Cu	Zn	Ga	Ge	As	Se	Br	Kr

Electron configurations of *d*-block elements

The 4s-subshell is at a lower energy level than the 3d-subshell and therefore the 4s-subshell fills before the 3d-subshell (Table 10). The orbitals in the 3d-subshell are first occupied singly to prevent any repulsion caused by pairing.

Table 10 Filling the 4s- and 3d-subshells

		4s	3d				
Sc	[Ar] $3d^1\,4s^2$	⇅	↑				
Ti	[Ar] $3d^2\,4s^2$	⇅	↑	↑			
V	[Ar] $3d^3\,4s^2$	⇅	↑	↑	↑		
Cr	[Ar] $3d^5\,4s^1$ *	↑	↑	↑	↑	↑	↑
Mn	[Ar] $3d^5\,4s^2$	⇅	↑	↑	↑	↑	↑
Fe	[Ar] $3d^6\,4s^2$	⇅	⇅	↑	↑	↑	↑
Co	[Ar] $3d^7\,4s^2$	⇅	⇅	⇅	↑	↑	↑
Ni	[Ar] $3d^8\,4s^2$	⇅	⇅	⇅	⇅	↑	↑
Cu	[Ar] $3d^{10}\,4s^1$ **	↑	⇅	⇅	⇅	⇅	⇅
Zn	[Ar] $3d^{10}\,4s^2$	⇅	⇅	⇅	⇅	⇅	⇅

*Chromium has one electron in each orbital of the 4s- and 3d-subshells, giving the configuration [Ar] $3d^5\,4s^1$, which is more stable than [Ar] $3d^4\,4s^2$.

**Copper has a full 3d-subshell, giving the configuration [Ar] $3d^{10}\,4s^1$, which is more stable than [Ar] $3d^9\,4s^2$.

The majority of transition elements form ions in more than one oxidation state. When transition elements form ions they do so by losing electrons from the 4s-orbitals before the 3d-orbitals. Sc and Zn each form ions in one oxidation state only, Sc^{3+} and Zn^{2+}. The electron configurations of these ions are shown as [Ar] $3d^0$ and [Ar] $3d^{10}$ respectively, such that neither fits the definition of a transition element.

Typical properties of transition elements

The transition elements are all metals and, therefore, they are good conductors of heat and electricity.

Variable oxidation states

Transition elements have compounds with two or more oxidation states (Table 11). This is primarily due to the fact that successive ionisation energies of transition

Exam tip

Most students get the full electron configuration of a transition metal correct. However, when asked for the electron configuration of a transition metal *ion* many incorrectly remove the 3d electrons before the 4s. The electron configuration of $_{26}Fe^{2+}$ is $1s^2\,2s^2\,2p^6\,3s^2\,3p^6\,3d^6$, not $1s^2\,2s^2\,2p^6\,3s^2\,3p^6\,4s^2\,3d^4$.

metals only increase gradually. All the transition metals can form an ion of oxidation state +2, representing the loss of the two $4s$-electrons. The maximum oxidation state possible cannot exceed the total number of $4s$- and $3d$-electrons in their electron configuration. (Once these electrons have been lost the stable electron configuration of argon is reached.)

Table 11

Common oxidation states of transition elements							
Ti	V	Cr	Mn	Fe	Co	Ni	Cu
+4, +3, +2	+5, +4, +3, +2	+6, +3, +2	+7, +6, +4 +3, +2	+3, +2	+3, +2	+3, +2	+2, +1

Colour of compounds

The transition elements have at least one oxidation state in which their compounds and ions are coloured. The colours are often distinctive and can be used as a means of identification. $Cu^{2+}(aq)$ ions are blue, $Cr^{3+}(aq)$ ions are green, $Cr_2O_7{}^{2-}(aq)$ are orange while $MnO_4{}^-(aq)$ ions are purple.

Catalysis

Transition metals are frequently used as heterogeneous catalysts. This is a result of the use of their d-orbitals to bind other molecules or ions to their surface. Examples include the use of iron as a catalyst in the Haber process to produce ammonia, the use of platinum, palladium and rhodium in the catalytic converter of a car and the use of nickel in the hydrogenation of alkenes. $MnO_2(s)$ also catalyses the decomposition of H_2O_2 into H_2O and O_2.

Ligands and complex ions

Transition metal ions are small and densely charged and can strongly attract electron-rich species called **ligands**, forming **complex ions** (Figure 30).

Common ligands include H_2O:, :Cl^-, :NH_3 and :CN^-, all of which have at least one lone pair of electrons.

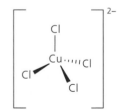

Octahedral (blue)   Tetrahedral (yellow)

Figure 30

In $[Cu(H_2O)_6]^{2+}$ the six electron pairs surrounding the central Cu^{2+} ion repel one another as far apart as possible and the complex ion has an octahedral shape such that all the bond angles are 90°.

In $[CuCl_4]^{2-}$ the four electron pairs surrounding the central Cu^{2+} ion repel one another so that they are as far apart as possible, and the complex ion has a tetrahedral shape such that all the bond angles are 109°28′ (109.5°).

Knowledge check 34

Deduce the oxidation number of the transition element in each of the following:
a $[Zn(NH_3)_4(H_2O)_2]^{2+}$
b $[Fe(CN)_6]^{4-}$
c $[Co(NH_3)_5Cl]^{2+}$
d $[Co(C_2O_4)_3]^{4-}$
e $[Cr(CH_3COO)_2(H_2O)_2]^+$

A **ligand** is defined as a molecule or ion that bonds to a metal ion forming a coordinate (dative covalent) bond by donating a lone pair of electrons into a vacant d-orbital.

A **complex ion** is defined as a central metal ion surrounded by (or coordinated with) ligands.

Exam tip

It is easy to lose marks by drawing a complex ion carelessly, showing the coordinate (dative) bond going from the wrong atom. In H_2O, the bond always goes from the O and not the H; in NH_3 the bond always goes from the N.

Coordination number

The **coordination number** of a transition metal, together with the number of lone pairs of electrons, defines the shape of a molecule or ion.

Complex ions with ligands such as H_2O and NH_3 are usually **6** coordinate and **octahedral** in shape. Complex ions with Cl^- ligands are usually **4** coordinate and **tetrahedral** in shape.

Ligands form a dative coordinate bond with a central transition metal ion. Some ligands are able to form two dative coordinate bonds with the central transition metal ion and are known as **bidentate ligands**.

1,2-diaminoethane is a common bidentate ligand (Figure 31). Each N has a lone pair of electrons and each can form a dative bond.

Figure 31

For example, a nickel complex could be drawn as shown in Figure 32.

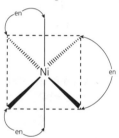

Figure 32

Stereoisomerism in complex ions

Isomerism is commonplace in organic compounds but it can also occur with some inorganic substances.

The square planar structure of $Ni(NH_3)_2Cl_2$ has two different isomeric forms with the ammonia molecules or chloride ions either being on opposite sides of the complex ion (the *trans* form) or alongside each other (the *cis* form) (Figure 33).

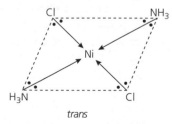 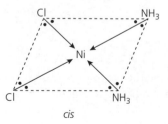

trans   *cis*

Figure 33

The **coordination number** is the total number of coordinate bonds from the ligands to the central transition metal ion in a complex ion.

Deduce the coordination number of the transition element in each of the following:
a $[Zn(NH_3)_4(H_2O)_2]^{2+}$
b $[Ag(NH_3)_2]^+$
c $[Co(NH_3)_5Cl]^{2+}$
d $[Co(H_2NCH_2CH_2NH_2)_3]^{3+}$

Exam tip

Any ion or molecule that has two nitrogens can act as a bidentate ligand and form complexes like the $Ni(en)_3^{2+}$ complex shown in Figure 36. To draw the complex all you have to do is replace 'en' with whatever you are given in the question. Diols and dicarboxylic acids can also behave as bidentate ligands because the oxygen atoms have lone pairs of electrons.

Optical isomerism is also possible in the case of complexes coordinated by polydentate ligands. The nickel 1,2-diaminoethane ion (Figure 34) is an example.

$$en = H_2NCH_2CH_2NH_2$$

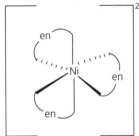

Figure 34

As is the case with organic molecules, it is the asymmetry of the structure that leads to this property and the two molecules shown cannot be superimposed on each other.

Complex ions have a variety of uses but one particularly interesting example is the *cis* form of the molecule $PtCl_2(NH_3)_2$. (The platinum is present as a 2^+ ion and the complex therefore has no overall charge.) The structure is shown in Figure 35.

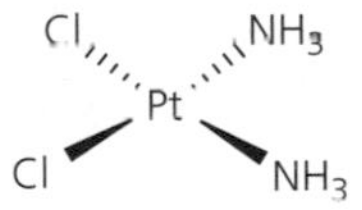

It is known as *cis*-platin and is used during chemotherapy as an anti-cancer drug. It is a colourless liquid that is usually administered as a drip into a vein and it works by binding to the DNA of cancerous cells and preventing their division. The importance of the exact shape and structure of the molecule is emphasised by the fact that the *trans* molecule is ineffective.

Ligand substitution

A ligand substitution reaction takes place when a ligand in a complex ion exchanges for another ligand.

Exchange between H₂O and NH₃ ligands

Water and ammonia ligands have similar sizes such that the coordination number does not change (Figure 36).

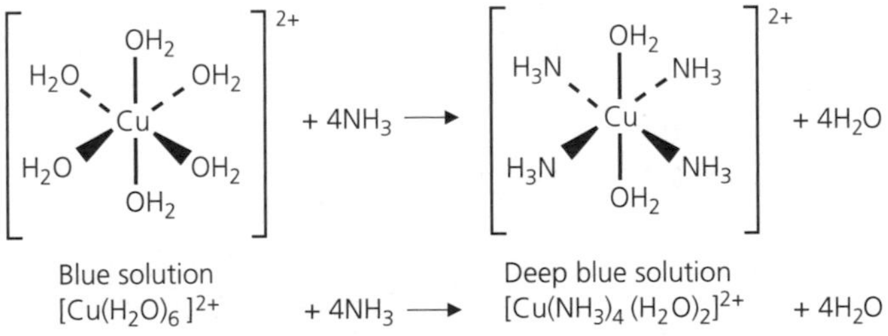

Figure 35

Knowledge check 36

Draw the stereoisomers of $[Co(NH_3)_4Cl_2]^+$ and $[Co(H_2NCH_2CH_2NH_2)_3]^{3+}$. In each case state the shape, the bond angles, the oxidation number of the transition metal ion and the type of isomerism.

$$\begin{bmatrix} & OH_2 & \\ H_2O & | & OH_2 \\ & Cu & \\ H_2O & | & OH_2 \\ & OH_2 & \end{bmatrix}^{2+} + 4NH_3 \longrightarrow \begin{bmatrix} & OH_2 & \\ H_3N & | & NH_3 \\ & Cu & \\ H_3N & | & NH_3 \\ & OH_2 & \end{bmatrix}^{2+} + 4H_2O$$

Blue solution $\qquad\qquad$ Deep blue solution
$[Cu(H_2O)_6]^{2+} \quad + 4NH_3 \longrightarrow \quad [Cu(NH_3)_4(H_2O)_2]^{2+} \quad + 4H_2O$

Figure 36

Exchange between H₂O and Cl⁻ ligands

Water molecules and chloride ions have *different* sizes and the coordination number changes (Figure 37).

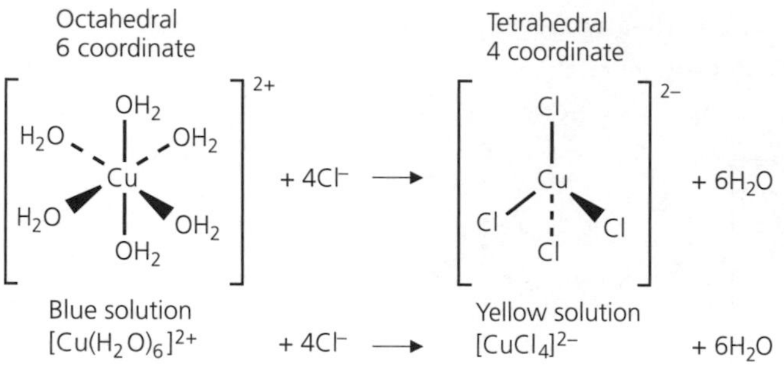

Octahedral
6 coordinate

Tetrahedral
4 coordinate

Blue solution
$[Cu(H_2O)_6]^{2+}$ $+ 4Cl^-$ $\longrightarrow$ Yellow solution
$[CuCl_4]^{2-}$ $+ 6H_2O$

Figure 37

Knowledge check 37

Write an equation for each of the following ligand-substitution reactions:

a $[Cu(H_2O)_6]^{2+} \rightarrow$ $[Cu(NH_3)_4(H_2O)_2]^{2+}$

b $[Co(NH_3)_6]^{3+} \rightarrow$ $[Co(NH_3)_5Cl]^{2+}$

c $[Fe(H_2O)_6]^{3+} \rightarrow$ $[Fe(H_2O)_5(SCN)]^{2+}$

A similar reaction takes place when Co^{2+} replaces Cu^{2+} such that $[Co(H_2O)_6]^{2+}$ (which is pink) can form $[CoCl_4]^{2-}$ (which is blue):

$$[Co(H_2O)_6]^{2+} + 4Cl^- \rightarrow [CoCl_4]^{2-} + 6H_2O$$

Simple precipitation reactions

A precipitation reaction takes place between aqueous alkali and an aqueous solution of a metal(II) or metal(III) cation. This results in the formation of a precipitate of the metal hydroxide, often with a characteristic colour. A suitable aqueous alkali is NaOH(aq). The colour of the precipitate can be used as a means of identification.

These precipitation reactions can be represented simply as follows:

$Cu^{2+}(aq) + 2OH^-(aq) \rightarrow Cu(OH)_2(s)$ Pale-blue precipitate

$Fe^{2+}(aq) + 2OH^-(aq) \rightarrow Fe(OH)_2(s)$ Pale-green gelatinous precipitate

$Fe^{3+}(aq) + 3OH^-(aq) \rightarrow Fe(OH)_3(s)$ Orange–brown gelatinous precipitate

$Fe(OH)_2(s)$ is slowly oxidised to $Fe(OH)_3(s)$ and, if left, the pale-green precipitate will change to orange–brown.

Other properties

Other properties of transition elements are that they are denser than other metals. They have smaller atoms than the metals in groups 1 and 2 such that the atoms are able to pack closely together, hence increasing the density. They also have higher melting and boiling points than other metals. This can also be explained by considering the size of the atoms of the transition elements. Within the metallic lattice, ions are smaller than those of the s-block metals, which results in greater 'free electron density' and hence a stronger metallic bond.

Redox reactions

Oxidation number

Oxidation number is a convenient way of quickly identifying whether or not a substance has undergone either oxidation or reduction. Many redox reactions take place in which transition metal ions change their oxidation state by *gaining* or *losing* electrons. Oxidation and reduction can be identified by either:

- movement of electrons — **o**xidation **is** the **l**oss of electrons; **r**eduction **is** the **g**ain of electrons ('OILRIG')
- change in oxidation state/number — oxidation is an increase in oxidation number, reduction is a decrease

The iron(II)–manganate(VII) reaction

The most common redox reaction involving transition elements is the reaction between $Fe^{2+}(aq)$ and $MnO_4^-(aq)$.

Step 1: write a half-ionic equation for each transition metal

In this reaction $Fe^{2+}(aq)$ changes to $Fe^{3+}(aq)$. This can be written as a half-ionic equation:

$$Fe^{2+} \rightarrow Fe^{3+} + 1e^- \qquad\qquad \text{Equation (1)}$$

Like any balanced equation the symbols and the charges have to balance. Fe^{2+} loses $1e^-$ when it is **oxidised** to Fe^{3+}.

If Fe^{2+} is oxidised, it follows that $MnO_4^-(aq)$ must be reduced. It is in fact reduced to Mn^{2+}. The first step in constructing a half-equation for this reduction is to recognise the change in oxidation state of the Mn. As oxygen is usually -2, it follows that in MnO_4^- the oxidation state of Mn is $+7$ and for Mn^{2+} the oxidation state of the Mn is $+2$. Therefore Mn changes from $+7$ to $+2$ and hence has to gain $5e^-$:

$$MnO_4^- + 5e^- \rightarrow Mn^{2+}$$

Clearly, this half-equation is *not* balanced. This reaction will not take place unless the MnO_4^- is acidified. Each O in the MnO_4^- forms a water molecule. Since there are four oxygens in MnO_4^-, four water molecules will be formed and hence eight H^+ are required:

$$MnO_4^- + 8H^+ + 5e^- \rightarrow Mn^{2+} + 4H_2O \qquad \text{Equation (2)}$$

Each half-equation is now balanced:

$$Fe^{2+} \rightarrow Fe^{3+} + 1e^- \qquad\qquad \text{Equation (1)}$$
$$MnO_4^- + 8H^+ + 5e^- \rightarrow Mn^{2+} + 4H_2O \qquad \text{Equation (2)}$$

Step 2: rewrite the half-equations so that the number of electrons in both is the same

In this case, we need to multiply equation (1) by 5 to get:

$$5Fe^{2+} \rightarrow 5Fe^{3+} + 5e^-$$

and

$$MnO_4^- + 8H^+ + 5e^- \rightarrow Mn^{2+} + 4H_2O \text{ (stays as before)}$$

Step 3: add the last two half-equations together to cancel out the electrons

So the actual reaction equation is:

$$5Fe^{2+} + MnO_4^- + 8H^+ \rightarrow 5Fe^{3+} + Mn^{2+} + 4H_2O$$

You can double-check the final equation is correct by making sure that the charges on each side balance.

Redox titrations

Transition metal ions are often coloured and the colour changes can be used to show when a titration has reached its end point. The reaction of Fe^{2+} with MnO_4^- is a good example of this. MnO_4^- is purple, while Mn^{2+} is pale pink or colourless. The purple MnO_4^- is added from a burette into acidified Fe^{2+} and it immediately turns pale pink–colourless as the MnO_4^- reacts with the acidified Fe^{2+}. When all of the Fe^{2+} has reacted, the purple colour of the MnO_4^- will remain. The end point of this titration is when a faint permanent pink colour can be seen.

The reaction between Fe^{2+} and MnO_4^- is often tested in the context of a titration calculation.

Example

Five iron tablets with a combined mass of 0.900 g were dissolved in acid and made up to 100 cm³ of solution. In a titration, 10.0 cm³ of this solution reacted exactly with 10.4 cm³ of 0.0100 mol dm⁻³ potassium manganate(VII). What is the percentage by mass of iron in the tablets?

Answer

Step 1: use the balanced equation

$$5Fe^{2+}(aq) + MnO_4^-(aq) + 8H^+(aq) \rightarrow 5Fe^{3+}(aq) + Mn^{2+}(aq) + 4H_2O(l)$$

Use the balanced equation to obtain the mole ratio of $Fe^{2+}:MnO_4^- = 5:1$. Calculate the number of moles of MnO_4^- by using the concentration and the reacting volume of $KMnO_4$. From the titration results, the amount of $KMnO_4$ can be calculated as:

$$c \times \frac{V}{1000} = 0.0100 \times \frac{10.4}{1000} = 1.04 \times 10^{-4}\,mol$$

From the mole ratio, the amount of Fe^{2+} can be determined:

$Fe^{2+} : MnO_4^-$

5 : 1

? : $1.04 \times 10^{-4}\,mol$

so, $5 \times 1.04 \times 10^{-4}\,mol\ Fe^{2+}$ reacts with $1.04 \times 10^{-4}\,mol\ MnO_4^-$

$$= 5.20 \times 10^{-4}\,mol$$

Step 2: find the amount of Fe^{2+} in the solution prepared from the tablets

10.0 cm³ of $Fe^{2+}(aq)$ contains $5.20 \times 10^{-4}\,mol\ Fe^{2+}(aq)$. So, 100 cm³ of the iron tablet solution contains:

$$10 \times (5.20 \times 10^{-4}) = 5.20 \times 10^{-3}\,mol\ Fe^{2+}$$

Step 3: Find the percentage of Fe^{2+} in the tablets

(A_r: Fe, 55.8)

$5.20 \times 10^{-3}\,mol\ Fe^{2+}$ has a mass of $5.20 \times 10^{-3} \times 55.8 = 0.290\,g$.

Therefore, the % of Fe^{2+} in the tablets is:

$$\frac{\text{mass of } Fe^{2+}}{\text{mass of tablets}} \times 100 = \frac{0.290}{0.900} \times 100 = 32.2\%$$

You also need to know a second redox titration between iodine and thiosulfate ions:

$$2S_2O_3^{2-}(aq) + I_2(s) \rightarrow S_4O_6^{2-}(aq) + 2I^-(aq) \qquad \text{Equation (1)}$$

This is not usually used directly to determine the concentration of an iodine solution, but instead it allows the determination of the concentration of a reagent that generates iodine as a result of a reaction.

An example is determination of the concentration of a copper sulfate solution. A known volume of copper sulfate is reacted with excess of potassium iodide and the following reaction occurs:

$$2Cu^{2+}(aq) + 4I^-(aq) \rightarrow Cu_2I_2(s) + I_2(s) \qquad \text{Equation (2)}$$

Cu_2I_2 is copper(I) iodide and it forms as a grey–white precipitate. The reaction is therefore a redox process, with the Cu^{2+} being reduced and the I^- being oxidised. The iodine produced is then titrated against a solution of sodium thiosulfate of known concentration.

At the start of the titration, the solution appears brown–purple as a result of the presence of the iodine but as the titration proceeds this colour fades to yellow and the end point is reached when the solution is colourless. The colour change is, in practice, quite hard to see clearly, especially as the precipitate of copper(I) iodide tends to get in the way. To help, some starch solution can be added as the end point is approached. This gives a dark blue coloration, which disappears more sharply at the end point.

It can be seen that from:
- equation (2), 2 mol of Cu^{2+} react to produce 1 mol of I_2
- equation (1), the 1 mol of I_2 reacts with 2 mol of $S_2O_3^{2-}$

It follows therefore that for every 1 mol of Cu^{2+}, 1 mol of $S_2O_3^{2-}$ is required. So the amount, in moles, of thiosulfate used is equivalent to the amount, in moles, of copper ion that was present.

Qualitative analysis

During your A-level course you have met several reactions that can be used to identify the presence of particular ions. The chemistry of the reactions is covered in the relevant sections of the books, but Table 12 summarises the identification tests that you need to know.

Knowledge check 38

0.426 g of a copper(II) salt is added to 25.0 cm³ KI(aq). The iodide is in excess. The I_2(aq) produced requires 18.0 cm³ of a 0.100 mol dm⁻³ solution of $S_2O_3^{2-}$(aq). Calculate the percentage of copper in the original salt. Quote your answer to an appropriate number of significant figures.

Table 12

Ion	Identification test
CO_3^{2-}	Add a dilute acid, bubbling occurs and a gas is given off. $2H^+(aq) + CO_3^{2-}(aq) \rightarrow H_2O(l) + CO_2(g)$ If the gas is collected and bubbled through limewater, $Ca(OH)_2(aq)$, a white precipitate of calcium carbonate, $CaCO_3(s)$, is produced.
Cl^-, Br^- or I^-	Dissolve the suspected halide and add aqueous silver nitrate. A silver halide precipitate forms, which is white with the chloride, cream with the bromide and yellow with the iodide. The equation can be represented as: $Ag^+(aq) + X^-(aq) \rightleftharpoons AgX(s)$ The $AgCl(s)$ precipitate re-dissolves in dilute ammonia, the $AgBr(s)$ precipitate re-dissolves in concentrated ammonia, and the $AgI(s)$ precipitate will not re-dissolve in ammonia.
SO_4^{2-}	Dissolve the suspected sulfate and add aqueous barium nitrate. A white precipitate of barium sulfate forms, which is insoluble in dilute nitric acid. $Ba^{2+}(aq) + SO_4^{2-}(aq) \rightarrow BaSO_4(s)$
NH_4^+	Warm the suspected ammonium compound with dilute aqueous sodium hydroxide. The smell of ammonia is apparent but can be tested with moist red litmus paper, which will turn blue as aqueous ammonia is alkaline. $NH_4^+(aq) + OH^-(aq) \rightleftharpoons NH_3(g) + H_2O(l)$
Cu^{2+}	Dissolve the suspected compound and add dilute aqueous ammonia. A light blue precipitate forms, which re-dissolves and forms a deep blue solution when excess ammonia is added. $Cu^{2+}(aq) + 2OH^-(aq) \rightarrow Cu(OH)_2(s)$
Fe^{2+}	Dissolve the suspected compound and add aqueous sodium hydroxide. A green precipitate forms. $Fe^{2+}(aq) + 2OH^-(aq) \rightarrow Fe(OH)_2(s)$
Fe^{3+}	Dissolve the suspected compound and add aqueous sodium hydroxide. A rust-brown precipitate forms. $Fe^{3+}(aq) + 3OH^-(aq) \rightarrow Fe(OH)_3(s)$
Mn^{2+}	Dissolve the suspected compound and add aqueous sodium hydroxide. A very pale pink precipitate forms. $Mn^{2+}(aq) + 2OH^-(aq) \rightarrow Mn(OH)_2(s)$
Cr^{3+}	Dissolve the suspected compound and add aqueous sodium hydroxide. A green precipitate forms, which re-dissolves when excess sodium hydroxide is added. Chromium compounds will also give a green precipitate with dilute aqueous ammonia. The precipitate re-dissolves when excess ammonia is added. $Cr^{3+}(aq) + 3OH^-(aq) \rightarrow Cr(OH)_3(s)$

Knowledge check 39

Explain how you would use chemical tests to distinguish between solutions of:

a manganese chloride and manganese nitrate

b ammonium sulfate and ammonium nitrate

c copper(II) nitrate and chromium(III) nitrate

d iron(II) sulfate and iron(III) sulfate

e manganese(II) chloride and iron(II) chloride

Summary

Having revised **Transition elements** you should now have an understanding of:

- general properties of transition elements
- precipitation reactions
- ligands and complex ions
- ligand substitution reactions
- redox reactions and titrations
- qualitative analysis

Questions & Answers

Approaching the exams

There are six modules in the A-level (H342) specification. The table summarises the structure and content of the A-level exams.

	Component exam	Modules						Total marks/ time	Types of question
		1	2	3	4	5	6		
A-level	Periodic table, elements and physical chemistry	✓	✓	✓		✓		100 marks 2 hours 15 min	Multiple choice (15 marks) Short response and extended response (85 marks)
	Synthesis and analytical techniques	✓	✓		✓		✓	100 marks 2 hours 15 min	Multiple choice (15 marks) Short response and extended response (85 marks)
	Unified chemistry	✓	✓	✓	✓	✓	✓	70 marks 1 hour 30 min	Short response and extended response (70 marks)

Question types

Multiple-choice questions will be used in A-level Components 1 and 2. Multiple-choice questions need to be read carefully and there is often a misconception that these questions have to be done 'in your head'. That is not the case, as many multiple-choice questions require you to think and to work things out on paper — space will be provided on the question paper. For each of the questions there are four suggested answers; A, B, C or D. You select your response by putting a cross in the box by the letter of your choice. Multiple-choice questions are machine-marked so it is essential that you follow the instructions given on the exam paper. The multiple-choice questions in this book will not be machine-marked and therefore do not follow the exam format exactly.

Short-response questions will appear in all exams at A-level. Read the questions carefully and be aware of the marks awarded for each section — for example, if there are 2 marks for a sub-section in a question you will be expected to make two points. The space provided for the answer has been designed to be more than sufficient for a complete response. Do not write in the margins. If you do require additional space, ask for extra paper and explain on the question paper that you have used extra paper for this response. Typical short-response questions are illustrated in this book by Q11–Q18.

Extended-response questions will appear in all component exams. Students often think of these types of question as 'essay' questions, but you do not have to use an essay style when answering these questions. Chemists communicate in a variety of ways, such as formulae, equations and mechanisms, all of which are difficult to put into an essay style. It is perfectly acceptable to use bullet points or to tabulate your response. Extended-response questions require that you plan your answer carefully.

Make sure that you use the marks allocated as guidance — if there are 8 marks you must make eight separate points. Check the mark schemes from previous papers and you will see that each mark is allocated to a specific point. Typical extended response questions are illustrated in this book by Q19–Q21.

Terms used in the exams

You will be asked precise questions in the examinations, so you can save a lot of valuable time — as well as ensuring that you score as many marks as possible — by knowing what is expected. Terms most commonly used are explained below.

Define: this requires a precise statement.

Explain: this normally implies that a definition should be given, together with some relevant comment on the significance or context of the term(s) concerned, especially where two or more terms are included in the question. The mark allocation should be used as a guide to how much supplementary comment is required.

State: this implies a concise answer with little or no supporting argument.

Describe: this requires students to state in words (using diagrams where appropriate) the main points of the topic. It is often used with reference to mechanisms and requires a step-by-step breakdown of the reaction including, where appropriate, curly arrows to show the movement of electrons. The mark allocation should be used as a guide to the amount of description required.

Deduce/predict: this implies that students are not expected to produce the required answer by recall but by making a logical connection between other pieces of information. Such information may be wholly given in the question or may depend on answers extracted in an earlier part of the question. 'Predict' also implies a concise answer with no supporting statement required.

Outline: this implies brevity, i.e. restricting the answer to giving essential detail only.

Suggest: this is used in two main contexts. It may either imply that there is no unique answer or that students are expected to apply their general knowledge to a novel situation — one that may not be referred to in the specification.

Calculate: this is used when a numerical answer is required. In general, working should be shown.

Sketch: when applied to diagrams, this implies that a simple, freehand drawing is acceptable. Nevertheless, care should be taken over proportions and the important details should be clearly labelled.

About this section

This section contains questions similar in style to those you can expect to see in your Component 1 and 3 exam papers.

Component 1 assesses content from Modules 1, 2, 3 and 5 and accounts for 37% of the total marks, with a written examination that is worth 100 marks. The exam lasts 2 hours 15 minutes and contains synoptic assessment, as well as stretch-and-challenge questions.

Component 3 assesses content from all modules and accounts for 26% of the total marks, with a written exam that is worth 70 marks. With synoptic assessment you must expect the questions to relate back to areas covered in the other modules. The stretch-and-challenge questions are designed to test the most able students when awarding the new A* grade.

The questions that follow give you a flavour of the types of questions that you will be asked, but it is impossible to cover all the topics and all the question styles. A more extensive range of questions is available in the OCR A2 Chemistry textbook published by Philip Allan, which also contains sections on stretch and challenge. Potential A*-grade students should practise answering these questions.

Comments on the questions are preceded by the icon ⓔ. They offer tips on what you need to do in order to gain full marks. All student responses are followed by additional comments, indicated by the icon ⓔ, which highlight where credit is due. In the weaker answers, they also point out areas for improvement, specific problems and common errors such as lack of clarity, irrelevance, misinterpretation of the question and mistaken meanings of terms.

Multiple-choice questions

Answer the questions that follow and record your answers. Check your answers when you have completed all ten questions.

Question 1

A substance has a concentration of $4.0 \, mol \, dm^{-3}$. Its decomposition is first order. If the half-life for this decomposition is $100 \, s$, how long would it take it to decompose until its concentration was $0.25 \, mol \, dm^{-3}$?

A $1600 \, s$

B $800 \, s$

C $400 \, s$

D $200 \, s$

Question 2

The rate at which equilibrium is established is affected by all of the following **except**:

A decreasing the temperature

B the presence of a catalyst

C decreasing the concentration of the reactants

D the equilibrium constant

Question 3

An equilibrium $X(g) \rightleftharpoons 2Y(g)$ has a value for $K_c = 1\,mol\,dm^{-3}$. This will mean that at equilibrium:

A $[X] = 2[Y]$

B $[X] = [Y]$

C $[X] = [Y]^2$

D $[X] = [Y]^{1/2}$

Question 4

The pH of a $0.001\,mol\,dm^{-3}$ sodium hydroxide solution is:

A 3

B 10

C 11

D 12

Question 5

Which one of the following equations represents the 2nd ionisation enthalpy of 1 mol of potassium ions?

A $K(s)$ $\rightarrow$ $K^{2+}(s) + e^-$

B $K(g)$ $\rightarrow$ $K^{2+}(g) + e^-$

C $K^+(s)$ $\rightarrow$ $K^{2+}(s) + e^-$

D $K^+(g)$ $\rightarrow$ $K^{2+}(g) + e^-$

Question 6

An exothermic reaction that has a negative value for its entropy change is:

A always feasible

B never feasible

C more feasible at low temperatures

D more feasible at high temperatures

Question 7

Which of the following pairs of atoms do **not** have the same number of $4s$ electrons?

A K and Cr

B Ca and Sc

C Cu and Mn

D Fe and Zn

Use the key below to answer questions 8, 9 and 10

A	B	C	D
1,2 and 3 correct	1,2 correct	2,3 correct	3 only correct

Question 8

Primary haloalkanes react with hydroxide ions to form an alcohol. The rate of reaction is first order with respect to both the primary haloalkane and the hydroxide ion. Which of the following apply to this reaction?

1 Doubling the concentration of one of the reagents will double the rate of the reaction.

2 Trebling the concentration of both reagents will increase the rate of the reaction nine fold.

3 Raising the temperature will increase the rate constant, k.

Question 9

Which of the following could **not** be used as the salt bridge when determining the electrode potential of $Ba^{2+}(aq)/Ba(s)$?

1 aqueous potassium nitrate

2 aqueous potassium chloride

3 aqueous potassium sulfate

Question 10

In which of the following reactions does nitric acid act as an acid?

1 $HNO_3 + HF \rightarrow H_2NO_3^+ + F^-$

2 $HNO_3 + H_2SO_4 \rightarrow NO_2^+ + 2HSO_4^- + H_3O^+$

3 $HNO_3 + HCOOH \rightarrow HCOOH_2^+ + NO_3^-$

Answers to multiple-choice questions

The student answers are all incorrect and are used to illustrate the most common incorrect response.

	1	2	3	4	5	6	7	8	9	10
Student answers	A	A	A	A	B	A	A	B	A	B
Correct answers	C	D	C	C	D	C	C	A	D	D

ⓔ It should now be apparent that you cannot answer all multiple-choice questions in your head. Many of the questions require working out on paper.

Q1 4 divided by 0.25 = 16 so it is easy to assume that it might take 16 × 100 s.

Q2 It is easy to misread the question. Many students interpret 'affects the rate' as increasing the rate.

Q3 It is easy to see why students would go for option A — you must write out the expression for K_p and then it is easy to see that option C is correct.

Q4 To calculate the pH of a base you must use K_w — not just –log the concentration.

Q5 Options A and B have been deliberately put there to tempt students to opt for the wrong answer and to not read *all* of the question carefully.

Q6 Students often assume that exothermic reactions are feasible but you really must use the Gibbs equation to determine the correct response.

Q7 All transition metal atoms, except Cr and Cu, have two $4s$ electrons.

Q8 The rate constant, despite the name *constant*, is only constant at a fixed temperature.

Q9 A salt bridge can be made using an ionic compound. However, K_2SO_4(aq) would precipitate with the Ba^{2+} ions and prevent movement of ions through the salt bridge.

Q10 Make use of the definitions — an acid is a proton donor, so look for NO_3^- as a product.

Short-response questions

Question 11 The rate equation

The reaction between hydrogen and nitrogen monoxide is a redox reaction and results in the formation of nitrogen and water.

(a) **(i)** Write a balanced equation for the reaction. (1 mark)

    (ii) Identify the oxidising agent in the reaction. Justify your answer. (2 marks)

(b) The rate equation for the reaction is: rate = $k[H_2(g)][NO(g)]^2$.

Using 1.2×10^{-2} moldm^{-3} H_2(g) and 6.0×10^{-3} moldm^{-3} NO(g), the initial rate of this reaction was 3.6×10^{-2} moldm^{-3}s^{-1}. Calculate the rate constant, k, for this reaction. Quote your answer to 2 significant figures. State the units of the rate constant, k. (4 marks)

(c) Calculate the initial rate of reaction when each of the following changes is made. Show your working.

    (i) The concentration of the H_2 is tripled. (1 mark)

    (ii) The concentration of the NO is halved. (1 mark)

    (iii) The concentration of both is doubled. (1 mark)

(d) Dinitrogen pentoxide decomposes according to the equation:

$2N_2O_5(g) \rightarrow 4NO_2(g) + O_2(g)$

The decomposition is a first-order reaction with respect to N_2O_5(g).

This decomposition proceeds by a two-step mechanism with the rate-determining step taking place first.

    (i) Write a rate equation for this reaction. (1 mark)

    (ii) Explain the term 'rate-determining step'. (1 mark)

    (iii) Suggest the two steps for this reaction and write their equations.

        Show clearly that the two steps equate to the balanced equation given above. (3 marks)

Total: 15 marks

🄔 The command word 'calculate' occurs many times in Component 1 and 3 examinations because much of the content is suitable for testing by calculations. In (b) and (c), calculate requires a numerical approach. If more than 1 mark is allocated, as in (b), it is essential to show your working, as any errors in the calculation will be marked consequentially. Therefore, provided that you show your working, incorrect answers may score some marks. Do not forget to follow the instructions relating to significant figures.

The command word 'suggest' in part (d) indicates that you have to use your knowledge and apply it to a problem that may not be on the specification.

Student A

(a) (i) $2H_2 + 2NO \rightarrow N_2 + 2H_2O$

Student B

(a) (i) $H_2 + NO \rightarrow \frac{1}{2}N_2 + H_2O$

🄔 Both students gain the mark. The equation must be balanced and it is acceptable to use fractions.

Student A

(a) (ii)   The H_2 has been oxidised because its oxidation number has increased, therefore, the NO must have been the oxidising agent.

Student B

(a) (ii)   NO

🄔 There are only two possible answers, the oxidising agent must be either H_2 or NO, and therefore there is a 50:50 chance of guessing the answer. When questions like this are asked there are usually no marks for the correct answer. The marks are awarded for the explanation. Both students have given the correct answer but Student B has given no explanation and so fails to score. The explanation given by Student A scores both marks although it is not ideal. It would be better to include relevant oxidation numbers to support the answer. The oxidation number of N in NO is +2 and the oxidation number of N in N_2 is 0. Therefore the reduction in the oxidation number as a result of the reaction identifies NO as the oxidising agent.

A good exam tip is to immediately write the oxidation numbers above each element in the equation:

Oxidation numbers	0	+2 −2	0	+1 −2
	$2H_2$ +	$2NO$ $\rightarrow$	N_2 +	$2H_2O$

so that the changes can be seen easily.

Questions & Answers

Student A

(b) rate = $k[H_2(g)][NO(g)]^2$

$3.6 \times 10^{-2} = k(1.2 \times 10^{-2})(6.0 \times 10^{-3})^2$

$3.6 \times 10^{-2} = k(1.2 \times 10^{-2})(3.6 \times 10^{-5})$

$3.6 \times 10^{-2} = k(4.32 \times 10^{-7})$

$k = \dfrac{3.6 \times 10^{-2}}{4.32 \times 10^{-7}} = 83\,333.3 = 8.3 \times 10^4$ (to 2 sig. figs.)

Student B

(b) $3.6 \times 10^{-2} = k(1.2 \times 10^{-2})(6.0 \times 10^{-3})^2$

$3.6 \times 10^{-2} = k(1.2 \times 10^{-2})(36 \times 10^{-6})$

$3.6 \times 10^{-2} = k(43.2 \times 10^{-8})$

$k = \dfrac{3.6 \times 10^{-2}}{43.2 \times 10^{-8}} = 83\,333.3$

---

e Both students have calculated the correct numerical value but neither quotes the units for k and both, therefore, lose a mark. Units for the rate constant involve some thought and always carry 1 mark. The question also asks for the answer to 2 significant figures; Student B has ignored this and loses another mark. There is usually a question that tests understanding of significant figures, but by the time you have finished a calculation, it is easy to forget about them.

A mark might be awarded for the correct use of significant figures without a specific warning being made in the question. If this is the case, there is usually some leeway allowed but it is good practice always to consider the appropriate number of significant figures to be included in your answer. It is not difficult since all that is required is that the number of significant figures that you give is the same as the number of significant figures in the information that has been supplied. In this particular case you can see that all the data in the question are given to 2 significant figures.

Student A

(c) (i) rate triples

(ii) rate twice as slow

(iii) rate four times as fast

Student B

(c) (i) rate triples

(ii) rate half as fast

(iii) rate eight times as fast

---

e Both students get 1 mark for part (i) but neither gets part (ii) correct. If the concentration of NO is halved, then the rate will change by $(1/2)^2 = 1/4$. Student B gets 1 mark for part (iii). Overall the reaction is third order and if both concentrations are doubled, the rate will change by $(2)^3 = 8$.

Student A

(d) (i) rate = $k[N_2O_5]$

Student B

(d) (i) rate = $[N_2O_5]$

---

e Student A gets 1 mark. Student B has forgotten to include the rate constant, k, and loses the mark.

Student A

(d) (ii) The slowest step in the mechanism.

Student B

(d) (ii) The slowest step.

---

e Both students get the mark.

Student A

(d) (iii)

$1N_2O_5$		$\rightarrow$	$2NO_2$	+	O;	slow step (RDS)
O	+ $1N_2O_5$	$\rightarrow$	$2NO_2$	+	O_2;	fast step
$2N_2O_5$		$\rightarrow$	$4NO_2$	+	O_2;	balanced equation

Student B

(d) (iii) $1N_2O_5 \rightarrow N_2O_3 + O_2$

$N_2O_3 + N_2O_5 \rightarrow 4NO_2$

$2N_2O_5 \rightarrow 4NO_2 + O_2$

---

e Students find devising mechanisms difficult, but both students have given good answers and score full marks. Where a question says 'suggest' it means that the examiner is not expecting a particular answer but is seeing if the student can provide some idea that might be true. The exact mechanism is not relevant, and both students have used the information in the question to suggest valid alternatives.

ⓔ Overall, Student A scores 12 out of 15, which is grade-A standard. Student B is awarded 9 out of 15 — a grade C. With a little more care and better examination technique, this could easily turn into grade A.

Question 12 Equilibrium

Hydrogen and iodine react according to the equation:

$$H_2(g) + I_2(g) \rightleftharpoons 2HI(g) \qquad \Delta H = +53.0 \, kJ \, mol^{-1}$$

(a) State le Chatelier's principle   (1 mark)

(b) Use le Chatelier's principle to predict what happens to the position of the equilibrium when:

   (i)   the temperature is increased

   (ii) the pressure is increased

   (iii) a catalyst is used

   Justify each of your predictions.   (6 marks)

(c) Write an expression for K_c for the equilibrium. State the units, if any.   (2 marks)

(d) (i) When 0.18 mol of I_2 and 0.5 mol H_2 were placed in a 500 cm^3 sealed container and allowed to reach equilibrium, the equilibrium mixture was found to contain 0.010 mol of I_2. Calculate K_c.   (5 marks)

   (ii) Explain what would happen to the value of K_c if the experiment was repeated with the 500 cm^3 container being replaced by one with a volume of 1 dm^3.   (2 marks)

                                                                        Total: 16 marks

ⓔ The command word 'state' used in part (a) indicates that a brief answer is required with no supporting argument. The command word 'explain' in part (d) (ii) requires a statement and some justification to support that statement. This is also true in (b) where 2 marks are allocated for each sub-part — 1 mark for the prediction and 1 mark for justifying that prediction.

Student A

(a) When a system at equilibrium is subjected to a change, the system will move to try to minimise the effect of the change.

Student B

(a) When a system at equilibrium is subjected to a change in external conditions, the system will move to cancel the effect of the change.

ⓔ Student A scores the mark but Student B does not. le Chatelier's principle states clearly that the system responds to a change by trying to minimise the effect of that change. It cannot cancel out the change.

Student A

(b) (i) The equilibrium moves to the right because it favours the endothermic forward reaction.

(ii) No effect because there are an equal number of moles of gas on both sides.

(iii) By lowering the activation energy the H_2 and I_2 react more readily so that more HI is made. Therefore the equilibrium moves to the right.

Student B

(b) (i) More HI will be produced because heat is absorbed when the forward reaction takes place.

(ii) Speeds up the reaction because it increases the chance of a collision.

(iii) Speeds up the reaction by lowering the activation energy.

e Student A scores 4 out of 6. The prediction about the position of the equilibrium and the explanation in parts (i) and (ii) are correct. What Student A has written in part (iii) is partly correct but they have failed to realise that the catalyst also affects the reverse reaction such that the position of the equilibrium remains unchanged.

Student B gets 2 marks for part (i) but fails to score for parts (ii) and (iii). The responses in parts (ii) and (iii) relate to the rate of the reaction and not to the position of the equilibrium and therefore no marks can be awarded.

Student A

(c) $K_c = \dfrac{[HI]^2}{[H_2][I_2]}$
There are no units.

Student B

(c) $K_c = \dfrac{[HI]^2}{[H_2][I_2]}$
(no units)

e Both students get 2 marks.

Questions & Answers

(d) (i)

$$H_2(g) \quad + \quad I_2(g) \quad \rightleftharpoons \quad 2HI(g)$$

Initial mol	0.5	0.18	0
Final mol		0.010	

It follows that 0.17 mol of I_2 and therefore 0.17 mol of H_2 also reacted.

Hence the mol of H_2 left is 0.5 − 0.17 = 0.33 mol.

For each mol of I_2 and H_2 that react 2 mol of HI are formed, therefore the equilibrium amount of 2 × 0.17 = 0.34 mol. K_c is measured in terms of concentration, therefore each of the equilibrium amounts must be converted to $mol\,dm^{-3}$.

$I_2 = 0.01/0.5 = 0.02\,mol\,dm^{-3}$

$H_2 = 0.33/0.5 = 0.66\,mol\,dm^{-3}$

$HI = 0.34/0.5 = 0.68\,mol\,dm^{-3}$

$$K_c = \frac{(0.68)^2}{(0.02)(0.66)} = 35$$

(d) (i) $K_c = \dfrac{[HI]^2}{[H_2][I_2]}$

$[I_2] = 0.01\,mol$ and $[H_2] = 0.5 - 0.17 = 0.33$

$[HI] = 0.34$

$$K_c = \frac{0.34}{0.01 \times 0.33} = 103$$

ⓔ Student A has worked through the calculation systematically, obtained the correct answer and scores 5 marks. Student B has made progress but carelessness once again means that marks are lost. First, the use of '[ ]' indicates that a concentration is being stated. However, in this case the student is referring to an amount in mol so statements such as $[I_2] = 0.01$ mol must not be used. Student A wisely converts the amounts in mol into concentrations before calculating the equilibrium constant. Student B does not do so and also puts 0.34 instead of $(0.34)^2$. In fact, in this case, since the total number of particles does not change as a result of the reaction, the volume of the container does not matter and the correct answer would be obtained using the amount in moles. It is not clear that Student B understands this. The result is that Student B can be given no more than 3 marks.

> **Student A**
>
> **(d) (ii)** If the volume of the container is increased to $1\,dm^3$, the equilibrium constant must be calculated as:
>
> $$I_2 = \frac{0.01}{1} = 0.01\,mol\,dm^{-3}$$
>
> $$H_2 = \frac{0.33}{1} = 0.33\,mol\,dm^{-3}$$
>
> $$HI = \frac{0.34}{1} = 0.34\,mol\,dm^{-3}$$
>
> $$K_c = \frac{(0.34)^2}{(0.01)(0.33)} = 35$$
>
> Which seems to be the same as before.

> **Student B**
>
> **(d) (ii)** K_c will be half what it was $= \dfrac{103}{2} = 51.5$.

ⓔ Student A seems rather surprised by the result and perhaps does not fully understand why but nonetheless the response is correct and 2 marks are awarded.

Student B seems quite confused and the answer is perhaps just a guess. No marks can be given.

ⓔ Overall, Student A scores 14 out of 16 — a good mark. Student B has not revised this topic carefully enough and only scores 7, which is no more than D/E-grade standard.

Question 13 pH

(a) (i) A weak organic acid, HA, has the percentage composition by mass: C, 40%; H, 6.7%; O, 53.3%. Calculate the empirical formula of HA. (2 marks)

(ii) HA has a relative molecular mass of 60.0. What is its molecular formula? (1 mark)

(b) 1.20 g of HA was dissolved in $250.0\,cm^3$ water. Calculate the pH of the resulting solution.
Show all of your working. (K_a of HA $= 1.7 \times 10^{-5}\,mol\,dm^{-3}$) (5 marks)

(c) A $0.04\,mol\,dm^{-3}$ solution of HA was titrated with a $0.05\,mol\,dm^{-3}$ sodium hydroxide solution.

(i) Calculate the pH of the NaOH(aq). ($K_w = 1.0 \times 10^{-14}\,mol^2\,dm^{-6}$) (2 marks)

(ii) Calculate the volume of NaOH(aq) required to neutralise $25.0\,cm^3$ of solution HA. (3 marks)

(iii) Sketch a graph to show the change in pH during the titration. (4 marks)

(d) Indicators can be used to determine the end point of a titration. Which of the following would be most suitable for this titration. Justify your answer and suggest what you would see at the end point. (3 marks)

Indicator	Acid colour	pH range	Alkaline colour
Thymol blue (acid)	Red	1.2–2.8	Yellow
Bromocresol purple	Yellow	5.2–6.8	Purple
Thymol blue (base)	Yellow	8.0–9.6	Blue

Total: 20 marks

ⓔ When asked to sketch a graph as in part (c)(iii) a great deal of care is required and it is important to label the axes. Parts (b) and (c)(i) require calculation of the pH of the acid and base respectively; (c)(ii) requires calculation of the volume of base required to neutralise the acid. Each of these factors has to be taken into account when sketching the graph.

Student A

(a) (i) Empirical formula:

C : H : O

$$\frac{40}{12.0} : \frac{6.7}{1.0} : \frac{53.3}{16.0}$$

3.33 : 6.7 : 3.33

1 : 2 : 1 = CH_2O

(ii) CH_2O has a mass = 12.0 + 2.0 + 16.0 = 30.0

∴ empirical mass × 2 = molecular mass

∴ molecular formula = $C_2H_4O_2$

Student B

(a) (i) Molecular mass is 60.0.

C is 40% = 24 = 2C

H is 6.7% = 4.02 = 4H

O is 53.3% = 31.98 = 2O

So formula is $C_2H_4O_2$, which means empirical formula is CH_2O.

(ii) Molecular formula is $C_2H_4O_2$.

ⓔ Student A gets 3 marks. Student B has not answered the question in the order presented. The relative molecular mass is given in part (ii) but has been used by the student to answer part (i). This is not the correct way of handling this question and it could be that the student would gain only the mark for part (ii) (i.e. 1). The examiner *might* allow the marks for part (i) but it is certainly not a wise way of tackling this question.

Student A

(b) $K_a = \dfrac{[H^+][A^-]}{[HA]} = \dfrac{[H^+]^2}{[HA]}$

$\therefore [H^+]^2 = K_a \times [HA]$

$K_a = 1.7 \times 10^{-5}$, $[HA] = \dfrac{1.2}{60} = 0.02$

$\therefore [H^+]^2 = 1.7 \times 10^{-5} \times 0.02 = 3.4 \times 10^{-7}$

$H^+ = \sqrt{3.4 \times 10^{-7}} = 5.8 \times 10^{-4}$

$pH = -\log_{10}[H^+] = -\log_{10}(5.8 \times 10^{-4}) = 3.23$

Student B

(b) $pH = -\log_{10}\sqrt{K_a \times [HA]}$

$pH = 4.69$

---

e Such questions are difficult to mark because there are a number of valid ways of carrying out the calculation. The instructions ask the students to 'Show all of your working'. Neither of the students has the correct answer of pH = 2.93. Student A scores 4 out of 5; Student B scores only 1 mark.

Student A has shown all the working and it is therefore possible to see where any mistakes have been made. The only error made by Student A is in working out the concentration of HA. By using the value 1.2/60.0 = 0.02 the number of moles of HA in $250\,cm^3$ has been worked out but not the *concentration* of HA. The correct concentration is $0.08\,mol\,dm^{-3}$.

It is impossible to deduce where Student B has gone wrong and so the only mark that can be awarded is for quoting an equation, $pH = -\log_{10}\sqrt{K_d \times [HA]}$, which could he used to obtain the correct answer.

Try the calculation: remember that $K_a = 1.7 \times 10^{-5}$ and [HA] =0.08.

Student A

(c) (i) $K_w = [H^+][OH^-] = 1.0 \times 10^{-14}$

$\qquad [H^+][0.05] = 1.0 \times 10^{-14}$

$\qquad \therefore [H^+] = \dfrac{1.0 \times 10^{-14}}{0.05} = 2.0 \times 10^{-13}$

$\qquad pH = -\log_{10}[H^+] = -\log_{10} 2.0 \times 10^{-13} = 12.7$

Student B

(c) (i) $pOH = -\log_{10}[OH^-] = -\log_{10}(0.05) = 1.30$

$\qquad pH = 14 - pOH = 14 - 1.30 = 12.7$

---

e Both students score 2 marks. The methods adopted are different but both are valid and lead to the correct answer.

Student A

(c) (ii)   HA + NaOH → NaA + H₂O

1 mol : 1 mol

moles of HA = moles of NaOH, $n = cV = \dfrac{0.04 \times 25.0}{1000} = 0.001$

volume of NaOH = $V = \dfrac{n}{c} = \dfrac{0.001}{0.05} = 0.02\,\text{dm}^3 = 20\,\text{cm}^3$

Student B

(c) (ii) $\dfrac{0.04 \times 25.0}{0.05} = 20\,\text{cm}^3$

ⓔ Both students get all 3 marks but Student B is living dangerously by providing no explanation. It is vital to show your working in any calculation.

Student A

(c) (iii)

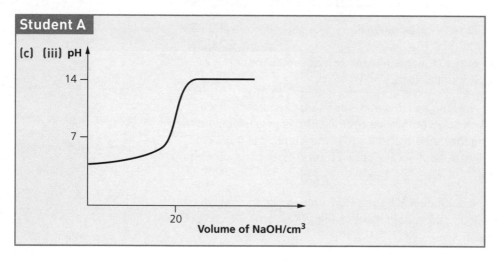

Student B

(c) (iii)

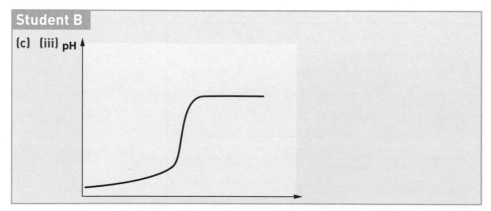

ⓔ The marking points for the sketch would be: correct labels, including units ✓, initial and final pH approximately correct ✓, correct shape ✓, rapid change in pH from about pH 7 to pH 12, after the addition of 20 cm³ of NaOH ✓.

Student A has been methodical and gains all 4 marks. Student B also understands the chemistry but only scores 2 marks. Use the mark scheme above and see if you can identify where Student B has lost 2 marks.

Student A

(d) Thymol blue (base) would be the best indicator because it changes colour in the pH region 8.0–9.6, which matches the rapid change in pH for this reaction.

Student B

(d) Thymol blue (base) would be the best indicator because it changes colour in the pH region 8.0–9.6. The end point would be a green colour.

ⓔ Both students have selected the correct indicator. Student A has given a good explanation of the choice of thymol blue (base) but has forgotten to say what would be seen at the end point. Student B has not explained why the indicator has been selected and has simply copied the pH range from the question. The end point should occur when there is an equal amount of the acid and the alkaline forms of the indicator, that is, an equal amount of yellow and blue, hence the end point would be green. Both students score 2 marks.

ⓔ **Both students seem to understand the chemistry, but Student B has failed to use this understanding well. Student A scores 18 out of 20; Student B only obtains 11 marks. The net result of poor technique is that Student B is underachieving by about two or three grades. Look back at Student B's responses and identify where marks could easily have been gained.**

Question 14 Acids, bases and buffers

A patient suffering from a duodenal ulcer displays increased acidity in their gastric juices. The exact acidity of the patient's gastric juice is monitored by measuring the pH.

(a) (i) Define pH. (1 mark)

   (ii) On one day the patient's gastric juice is found to have a hydrochloric acid concentration of $8.0 \times 10^{-2}\,\text{mol}\,\text{dm}^{-3}$. Calculate the pH of the gastric juice. (1 mark)

(b) One of the most common medications designed for the relief of excess stomach acidity is aluminium hydroxide, $Al(OH)_3$.

   (i) Write an equation for the reaction between HCl and $Al(OH)_3$. (1 mark)

   (ii) On another day the gastric juice of the patient is found to have a pH of 1.3. The patient produces $2\,\text{dm}^3$ of gastric juice in a day. This volume of gastric juice is to be treated with tablets containing $Al(OH)_3$ to raise the pH to 2.

   Calculate the mass of aluminium hydroxide required to raise the pH of $2\,\text{dm}^3$ of gastric juice from 1.3 to 2. (5 marks)

(c) The control of the pH of blood is also important. This is achieved by the presence of HCO_3^- ions in blood plasma. Using appropriate equations, explain how HCO_3^- can act as a buffer solution.

(3 marks)

Total: 11 marks

e The command word 'calculate' in parts (a)(ii) and (b)(ii) requires a numerical approach. In (b)(ii) it is important that you show your working as any errors in the calculation will be marked consequentially. The calculation accounts for almost half the marks in this question. Part (c) requires knowledge of the equilibrium involved along with an explanation of how the equilibrium counteracts changes in acidity and alkalinity.

Student A

(a) (i)   pH is minus the logarithm to base 10 of the hydrogen ion concentration in a solution.

Student B

(a) (i) $pH = -log[H^+]$

---

e Both students get the mark. Student A has made it harder to answer the question by defining pH in words. Some students seem to think that definitions should always be given in words. This is not the case and Student B has the better approach.

Student A

(a) (ii) $pH = -log_{10}(8.0 \times 10^{-2}) = 1.10$

Student B

(a) (ii) $pH = 1.097$

---

e Both students get the mark although both quoted their answers to too many significant figures. If the question had carried 2 marks, Student B, in particular, might have only scored 1.

Student A

(b) (i) $3HCl + Al(OH)_3 \rightarrow AlCl_3 + 3H_2O$

Student B

(b) (i) $3HCl + Al(OH)_3 \rightarrow AlCl_3 + 3H_2O$

---

e Both students get the mark.

Student A

(b) (ii) A pH of 2 means $[H^+] = 10^{-2}$ or $0.01\,mol\,dm^{-3}$

A pH of 1.3 means $[H^+] = 10^{-1.3} = 0.05\,mol\,dm^{-3}$

The pH has to be raised by $0.04\,mol$

$3HCl + Al(OH)_3 \rightarrow AlCl_3 + 3H_2O$

Therefore $0.04/3\,mol$ of $Al(OH)_3$ are needed $= 0.0133\,mol$

$1\,mol$ of $Al(OH)_3 = 78.0\,g$

So $Al(OH)_3$ needed is $0.0133 \times 78.0 = 1.04\,g$

Student B

(b) (ii) A pH of 2 is $0.01\,mol\,dm^{-3}$

A pH of 1.3 is $0.02\,mol\,dm^{-3}$

So $2\,dm^3$ of gastric juice has $0.04\,mol$ and must become 0.02 by adding $Al(OH)_3$

Using the equation gives mol of $Al(OH)_3$ of $0.02/3$

$Al(OH)_3 = 78.0\,g$

So $Al(OH)_3$ needed is $\dfrac{78.0 \times 0.02}{3} = 0.52\,g$

ⓔ This is quite a difficult question and is perhaps intended as one of the stretch-and-challenge parts that are included to test the best students. Although both students have obtained the wrong answer both have done well and achieved 4 out of the 5 marks.

In the mark scheme there is a mark each for converting the two pH values to concentrations of H^+. There is 1 mark for working out the amount, in mol, of H^+ that has to be neutralised. The fourth mark is for the moles of aluminium hydroxide required and the final mark for converting this into grams.

Student A forgets that the volume being treated is $2\,dm^3$ and so concludes that $0.04\,mol$ of HCl must be neutralised by the $Al(OH)_3$. The figure should be $0.08\,mol$ for the $2\,dm^3$. So the third mark is lost. After that the calculation is correct, so only 1 mark is dropped overall. The examiner will always award marks for later parts of a question if they are carried out correctly, even if an error has been made earlier. Student A makes a statement that is worded poorly. It is incorrect to write 'The pH has to be raised by $0.04\,mol$' instead of 'To raise the pH from 1.3 to 2 requires the amount, in moles, of H^+ to be changed from 0.05 to 0.01'. However, in a calculation the examiner is unlikely to be too hard on poor wording and it is better not to worry too much about it. Be careful, though, always to provide correct units for quantities as these might carry marks.

Student B fails to convert the pH of 1.3 to the correct concentration of hydrogen ions. This is a common error and often occurs because students have not learned how to use their calculators reliably. You should make certain that this does not happen to you. Although again rather poorly worded, this answer shows that Student B does remember that $2\,dm^3$ is being used and from this stage completes the calculation correctly.

Student A

(c) The addition of H^+ causes the HCO_3^- ion to convert to CO_2.

$HCO_3^- + H^+ \rightleftharpoons CO_2 + H_2O$

So this allows any excess acid to be partly controlled.

The addition of alkali converts the HCO_3^- to CO_3^{2-}.

$HCO_3^- + OH^- \rightleftharpoons CO_3^{2-} + H_2O$

This is not very likely in the blood though.

Student B

(c) The buffer works like:

$HCO_3^- + H^+ \rightleftharpoons CO_2 + H_2O$

$HCO_3^- + OH^- \rightleftharpoons CO_3^- + H_2O$

---

e Student A provides a satisfactory answer and, in particular, does well to mention that buffers only partly control the pH. A common error is to say that buffer solutions stop the pH from changing. This would always lose a mark as, although buffer solutions stabilise pH well, they cannot totally stop the pH from changing. Student A scores 3 marks.

Student B does not give any explanation and therefore loses 1 mark. The first equation is correct but the second has the carbonate ion as CO_3^-, which is a serious error at A2 and means that a second mark is lost. Therefore only 1 mark is obtained for this part of the question.

e **Overall, Student A scores 10 out of 11, an excellent mark. Student B gets 8 out of 11, which falls just short of grade-A standard because of careless errors.**

Question 15 Born–Haber and related energy cycles

(a) (i) Explain what is meant by the term lattice enthalpy. (2 marks)

    (ii) Write an equation to show what is meant by the lattice enthalpy of magnesium chloride. (2 marks)

(b) Use the Born–Haber cycle below to answer the questions that follow.

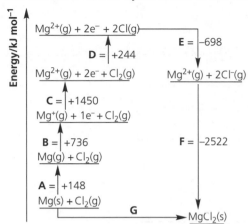

(i) Identify which step represents the second ionisation energy of magnesium. (1 mark)

(ii) Write an equation that illustrates the second ionisation energy of magnesium. (1 mark)

(iii) Explain why the enthalpy value for the second ionisation energy of magnesium is about twice the value of the first ionisation energy of magnesium. (2 marks)

(iv) Write an equation that illustrates the first electron affinity of chlorine. (2 marks)

(v) State the energy, in $kJ\,mol^{-1}$, for the first electron affinity of chlorine. (1 mark)

(vi) Calculate the enthalpy of formation of magnesium chloride. (2 marks)

(c) The lattice enthalpy for magnesium bromide is $-2440\,kJ\,mol^{-1}$.
Explain the difference in the values of the lattice enthalpies of magnesium bromide and magnesium chloride. (1 mark)

(d) Magnesium bromide is soluble in water.
The enthalpy of hydration of magnesium ions is $-1921\,kJ\,mol^{-1}$ and the enthalpy of hydration of the bromide ion is $-336\,kJ\,mol^{-1}$.
Calculate the enthalpy of solution of magnesium bromide. (2 marks)

(e) Using enthalpies of solution is not always a reliable way of predicting whether a substance will be soluble in water.

(i) What other energy change should be considered in making a prediction of solubility? (1 mark)

(ii) Explain whether this other energy change is likely to suggest that a substance will be more or less soluble in water. (2 marks)

(f) Describe how you could distinguish between aqueous solutions of magnesium bromide and magnesium chloride. State the observations you would make. (3 marks)

Total: 22 marks

ⓔ There are several parts in this question and each starts with a command word. It is important that you follow the instructions precisely. 'State' requires a brief answer with no supporting argument; 'explain' and 'describe' require more detailed answers with some additional comment.

Questions & Answers

Student A

(a) (i) The lattice enthalpy is the enthalpy change when 1 mol of ionic solid is formed from its ions in the gas state.

Student B

(a) (i) It is the enthalpy released when the constituent gaseous ions form 1 mol of ionic solid.

e Both score 2 marks. It is essential that you learn straightforward definitions. The marks in this definition are for: forming 1 mol of ionic solid ✓, from the gaseous ions ✓.

Student A

(a) (ii) $Mg^{2+}(g) + 2Cl^-(g) \rightarrow MgCl_2(s)$

Student B

(a) (ii) $Mg^{2+} + Cl_2^-(g) \rightarrow MgCl_2(s)$

e Student A gets both marks but Student B scores nothing.

Student B has not included the state symbol, (g), after Mg^{2+}. Many students forget to put state symbols in equations. In cases such as this, where a change in state is involved, they are essential. Do not be caught out by this.

Student B has also made another common error: $2Cl^-(g)$ is not the same as $Cl_2^-(g)$. Writing $Cl_2^-(g)$ implies that the two Cl are joined together and have made a Cl_2 molecule which has then received a '−' charge. This is incorrect; each Cl has received a '−' charge and so this must be written as $2Cl^-$.

Student A

(b) (i) C

Student B

(b) (i) C

e Both students get the mark.

Student A

(b) (ii) $Mg^+(g) \rightarrow Mg^{2+}(g) + 1e^-$

Student B

(b) (ii) $Mg(s) \rightarrow Mg^{2+}(g) + 2e^-$

ℯ Student A gets the mark and has made good use of the information in the question. Student B fails to score.

The equation given by Student B is incorrect on a number of counts. Most important is that the equation shows the first and second ionisation energies combined together. In addition, Student B has made another careless error in thinking of magnesium as a solid and adding this as the state symbol in the equation. He/she has forgotten that for the process of ionisation the magnesium has first been atomised and is therefore a gas.

Student A

(b) (iii) Mg^+ is smaller than the Mg atom and therefore it is more difficult to remove the second electron.

Student B

(b) (iii) The second ionisation energy removes two electrons but the first only one, therefore it is twice as much.

ℯ This is a difficult concept. The ease with which an electron can be removed depends on the attraction between the protons in the nucleus and the outer electrons. The three main factors that influence this are:

- distance from the nucleus
- shielding by inner shells
- proton to electron ratio

You must remember to consider all three factors to identify which of them might be relevant to the answer expected. The shielding remains constant for the first and second ionisation energies of Mg, but the distance from the nucleus and the proton:electron ratio both change. Student A scores 1 mark for explaining the variation in size/distance from the nucleus, but Student B fails to score. Student B has fallen for the trap set by the question and jumped to the wrong conclusion.

Student A

(b) (iv) $Cl(g) + 1e^- \rightarrow Cl^-(g)$

Student B

(b) (iv) $Cl(g) + e^- \rightarrow Cl^-(g)$

ℯ Both students get the mark.

Student A

(b) (v) $-698 \, \text{kJ} \, \text{mol}^{-1}$

Student B

(b) (v) 349

---

e Neither student gets the mark. Student A has used the information in the question but failed to spot that the enthalpy change given is for 2 × first electron affinity of chlorine. Student B has spotted this and has halved the numerical value but has forgotten to put in the negative sign and also has omitted to put units.

Student A

(b) (vi) $\Delta_f H = 148 + 736 + 1450 - 698 - 2522 = -642 \, \text{kJ} \, \text{mol}^{-1}$

Student B

(b) (vi) $-642 \, \text{kJ} \, \text{mol}^{-1}$

---

e Both students get 2 marks but Student A shows better examination technique by showing the working.

Although you should use a calculator to avoid making an error in the arithmetic, it is wise to write down your working. If you then make a mistake, the examiner can check whether a mark can still be awarded. It is surprising how often this turns out to be the case. Although a correct answer will normally score full marks, no mark will be awarded if there is an error and no working is shown. In some cases a question will specify that working *must* be shown and in this case marks are awarded specifically for the steps of the calculation.

Student A

(c) The lattice enthalpy depends on the ionic radius and the size of the charge. The charge for Cl^- and Br^- is the same but the Cl^- is smaller than the Br^- and therefore the attraction between the Mg^{2+} ion and the Cl^- will be greater.

Student B

(c) charge density of $Cl^- > Br^-$

Therefore the lattice enthalpy $MgCl_2$ is bigger than $MgBr_2$.

---

e Student A would definitely get the mark. Student B would probably score too, but he/she has not given a clear answer to the question. The fault lies in the use of the word 'bigger'. This is arguable because with lattice energies we are dealing with negative numbers. It is true that the numerical value of the lattice energy is greater for magnesium chloride than it is for magnesium bromide, but is -2522 bigger or smaller than -2440? In answering questions of this type where numbers are negative it is best to avoid saying that the lattice energy is just bigger, greater, more, less or smaller, and say instead that the numerical value of the lattice energy is either more or less negative.

Student A

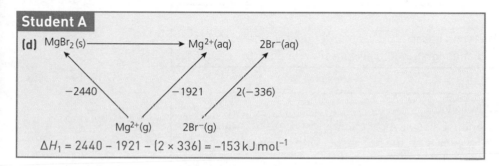

$\Delta H_1 = 2440 - 1921 - (2 \times 336) = -153\,\mathrm{kJ\,mol^{-1}}$

Student B

(d) Enthalpy of solution $= -2440 + 1921 + 672 = 153\,\mathrm{kJ\,mol^{-1}}$

---

e Student A gets both marks but Student B has made an error in the sign of the answer and therefore scores only 1 mark. In questions involving enthalpy changes it is always a good idea to provide a diagram indicating the direction of the enthalpy changes involved. It helps to avoid unnecessary errors.

Student A

(e) (i) The entropy change

Student B

(e) (i) Entropy

---

e Both students get the mark.

Student A

(e) (ii) Entropy increases when a substance dissolves in water as the particles can move more readily. This means that substances will be predicted to be more soluble than when just enthalpy is used.

> **Student B**
>
> (e) (ii) More soluble

ⓔ Student A scores the 2 marks but Student B fails to score as no explanation is provided.

If a question is asked to which the answer is 50:50 (i.e. in this case it could either be 'more' or 'less') no mark is available without an explanation.

> **Student A**
>
> (f) Add silver nitrate to each and observe the colour of the precipitate. $MgCl_2$ would give a white solid and $MgBr_2$ would give a yellow solid.

> **Student B**
>
> (f) Both solutions would conduct electricity. If electricity is passed through the $MgCl_2$ a green gas will be evolved at the anode, but with $MgBr_2$ an orange/brown liquid will be produced.

ⓔ This part of the question is synoptic: you have to recall information and knowledge from other areas of the specification. Student A has selected $AgNO_3$ as the reagent. This relates back to Module 3 (Periodic table and energy), where $AgNO_3$ is used to distinguish between the halides in the section on group 7. The observation for the chloride is correct but the colour for the bromide is incorrect. The iodide gives a yellow precipitate with $AgNO_3$ and the bromide gives a cream precipitate. Student A, therefore, gets 2 marks and perhaps is quite lucky not to lose a further mark for not specifying that the silver nitrate should be aqueous. When describing chemical tests you should always consider the state of the reagents as this could be included in the mark scheme.

Student B has given an unexpected answer, but nevertheless it is good chemistry and would probably work. Student B might get all 3 marks although it would be difficult to detect the chlorine by colour.

ⓔ Student A shows a good grasp of this topic and has been systematic in supplying the answers. Good use is made of the information in the question. The score of 18/22 is comfortably grade-A standard. Student B scores 12/22 — equivalent to a C grade — with marks lost mostly by carelessness.

Question 16 Enthalpy, entropy and free energy

(a) Use the data below to calculate the standard enthalpy change for the reaction:

$C(s) + CO_2(g) \rightarrow 2CO(g)$

$\Delta_f H^{\ominus} (CO_2) = -393 \, kJ \, mol^{-1}$

$\Delta_f H^{\ominus} (CO) = -110.5 \, kJ \, mol^{-1}$

(2 marks)

(b) Use the data below to calculate the standard entropy change for the reaction:
C(s) + CO₂(g) → 2CO(g)
$S^{\ominus}(CO_2) = 213.8\,J\,mol^{-1}\,K^{-1}$
$S^{\ominus}(C) = 5.7\,J\,mol^{-1}\,K^{-1}$
$S^{\ominus}(CO) = 197.9\,J\,mol^{-1}\,K^{-1}$ (2 marks)

(c) (i) State the relationship between ΔG, ΔH and ΔS. (1 mark)

(ii) Use your answers to (a) and (b) above to determine the value of $\Delta G^{\ominus}$ for the reaction of carbon dioxide and carbon under standard conditions of 298 K and 101 kPa. (2 marks)

(d) Calculate the minimum temperature in °C required for the reaction between carbon dioxide and carbon to become feasible. (3 marks)

Total: 10 marks

ℯ The command word 'calculate' features in parts (a), (b) and (d) and requires a numerical approach. In part (c)(ii) 'determine' also requires a numerical approach. Therefore 9 of the 10 marks in this question involve calculations.

Student A

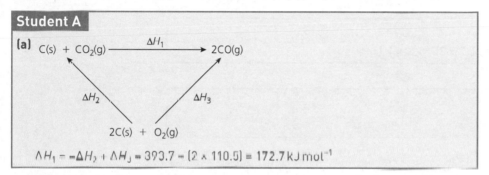

(a)
C(s) + CO₂(g) —— ΔH_1 —→ 2CO(g)

ΔH_2 ΔH_3

2C(s) + O₂(g)

$\Delta H_1 = -\Delta H_2 + \Delta H_3 = 393.7 - (2 \times 110.5) = 172.7\,kJ\,mol^{-1}$

Student B

(a) Enthalpy change = $-(2 \times 110.5) - (-393.7) = -172.7\,kJ\,mol^{-1}$

ℯ Although enthalpy cycles were studied in Module 3, they are clearly relevant to the study of free energies in Module 5. You must therefore be ready to complete calculations of this type.

Student A gets both marks. It is not a requirement that an enthalpy diagram is provided but it may help to avoid errors. Student B sees the enthalpy change as (enthalpy of the products) – (enthalpy of the reactants), which is fine, but the student has become muddled working out the answer and has ended up with the wrong sign for the answer. Only 1 mark is scored. It is all too easy to make this mistake so all calculations should be checked carefully. It is always worthwhile to look at the reaction and consider whether you expect it to be exothermic or endothermic.

Student A

(b) The entropy change is $2S^{\ominus}(CO) - S^{\ominus}(CO_2) - S^{\ominus}(C) = (2 \times 197.9) - 213.8 - 5.7$
$= 176.3\,kJ\,mol^{-1}$

> **Student B**
>
> (b) Change is $(2 \times 197.9) - 213.8 - 5.7 = 176.3\,J\,mol^{-1}\,K^{-1}$

ⓔ Both students have carried out the arithmetic correctly but Student A has incorrectly written the units as $kJ\,mol^{-1}$. Therefore Student A scores only 1 mark but Student B scores 2 marks.

> **Student A**
>
> (c) (i) $\Delta G = \Delta H - T\Delta S$

> **Student B**
>
> (c) (i) $\Delta G = \Delta H - T\Delta S$

ⓔ Both students get the mark.

> **Student A**
>
> (c) (ii) $\Delta G = 172.7 - (298 \times 0.1763) = 120.2\,kJ\,mol^{-1}$

> **Student B**
>
> (c) (ii) $\Delta G = -225.2\,kJ\,mol^{-1}$

ⓔ Student A has remembered to convert the entropy value from J into kJ and has completed the calculation correctly for 2 marks.

Student B has used the wrong answer obtained in part (a) and has then completed the calculation correctly. In general, the examiner allows marks for calculations that are incorrect, if they are based on an error in a previous part of the question that has already been penalised. If Student B had shown the working for the calculation, 2 marks would have been awarded. However, if the examiner cannot see how the answer has been obtained, these marks can be lost.

> **Student A**
>
> (d) For a reaction to be feasible $\Delta G = 0$, so $\Delta H = T\Delta S$
>
> $\qquad 172.7 = T(0.1763)$
>
> $\qquad T = 979°C$

Student B

(d) At equilibrium $\Delta H = T\Delta S$

$-172.7 = 0.1763T$

$T = -979$ or $-979 - 273 = -1252°C$

ⓔ Student A scores 2 out of the 3 marks as the answer given is in K and not °C. The correct answer is $979 - 273 = 706°C$. Student B is still suffering from the error made in part (a) but this time has shown the working of the calculation. It is all correct and, even though the answer is wrong, the examiner will award 3 marks. It is a pity that the student, once a clearly wrong answer had been obtained, did not check the arithmetic. However this may not have been possible if time was short. Sometimes students are tempted to cross out parts of questions where they have recognised that the answer cannot be right. This is a mistake because, as in this case, it might still be possible to get some credit for what is there.

ⓔ **Student A has dropped 2 marks and obtained 8 out of 10, which is grade-A standard, but it could have been full marks with just a little more care. Student B would perhaps have only scored 7. It could have been more if the examiner had recognised what had happened in part (c)(ii).**

Question 17 Redox equations and electrode potentials

(a) Draw a diagram to show how the standard electrode potential of the half-cell $Fe^{3+}(aq) + e^- \rightleftharpoons Fe^{2+}(aq)$ would be measured. State the conditions necessary. (6 marks)

(b) Use the following electrode potentials to predict whether, under standard conditions, $Fe^{3+}(aq)$ will be able to react with:

(i) $I^-(aq)$

(ii) $Br^-(aq)$

$I_2(aq) + 2e^- \rightleftharpoons 2I^-(aq)$	$E^\ominus = +0.54\,V$
$Fe^{3+}(aq) + e^- \rightleftharpoons Fe^{2+}(aq)$	$E^\ominus = +0.77\,V$
$Br_2(aq) + 2e^- \rightleftharpoons 2Br^-(aq)$	$E^\ominus = +1.09\,V$

If a reaction is possible, state what you would observe as the reaction took place. (5 marks)

(c) $I^-(aq)$ reacts with acidified $KMnO_4$ to form $Mn^{2+}(aq)$ ions and $I_2(aq)$.
Write half-equations for each of these reagents and use them to construct a balanced ionic equation for the reaction. (3 marks)

Total: 14 marks

ⓔ Part (a) requires a diagram but care is needed as 6 marks are available. Before starting, plan what you need to include for the 6 marks — the hydrogen electrode ✓, the Fe^{2+}/Fe^{3+} electrode ✓, the salt bridge and the voltmeter ✓, as well as the conditions of temperature ✓, pressure ✓ and the concentrations ✓ are all required.

Student A

(a) At 298 K and 100 kPa:

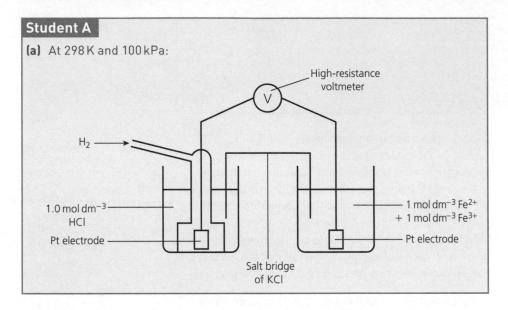

Student B

(a)

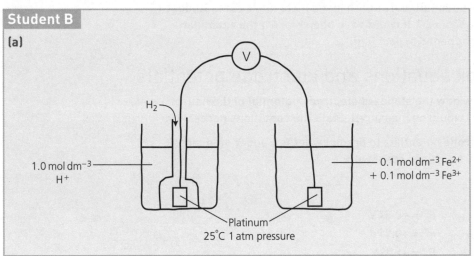

25°C 1 atm pressure

e To ensure no marks are lost, both students ought to include state symbols with each of the chemicals. Student A has learnt this topic well and scores all 6 marks. Student B knows the work quite well but has failed to include a salt bridge in the diagram. This loses 1 mark. The diagram is drawn poorly but so long as it is clear this will not lose marks. A good point about Student B's work is that the concentrations chosen for the $Fe^{2+}(aq)$ and $Fe^{3+}(aq)$ are more realistic than those of Student A. The value of the electrode potential measured will be the same for redox pairs such as $Fe^{2+}(aq)$ and $Fe^{3+}(aq)$ if their concentrations in $mol\,dm^{-3}$ are the same. The use of concentrations of $1\,mol\,dm^{-3}$ might be difficult if the compounds are not very soluble in water. However, no mark should be lost if the higher concentrations are suggested.

Student A

(b) (i) $I_2(aq) + 2e^- \rightleftharpoons 2I^-(aq)$ $E^\ominus = +0.54\,V$

$Fe^{3+}(aq) + e^- \rightleftharpoons Fe^{2+}(aq)$ $E^\ominus = +0.77\,V$

So the possible overall reaction would be:

$2Fe^{3+}(aq) + 2I^-(aq) \rightarrow I_2(aq) + 2Fe^{2+}(aq)$

$E^\ominus$ for this is $0.77 - 0.54 = 0.23\,V$ so the reaction is possible.

In the reaction you would see iodine formed.

(ii) $Br_2(aq) + 2e^- \rightleftharpoons 2Br^-(aq)$ $E^\ominus = +1.09\,V$

$Fe^{3+}(aq) + e^- \rightleftharpoons Fe^{2+}(aq)$ $E^\ominus = +0.77\,V$

So the possible overall reaction would be:

$2Fe^{3+}(aq) + 2Br^-(aq) \rightarrow Br_2(aq) + 2Fe^{2+}(aq)$

$E^\ominus$ for this is $0.77 - 1.09 = -0.32\,V$ so the reaction is not possible.

Student B

(b) (i) Possible equation is $2Fe^{3+}(aq) + 2I^-(aq) \rightarrow I_2(aq) + 2Fe^{2+}(aq)$

Overall $E^\ominus = 2 \times 0.77 - 0.54 = 1.00\,V$

So the reaction can take place and you will see the brown colour of iodine in solution and the yellow Fe^{3+} would go green.

(ii) Possible equation is $2Fe^{3+}(aq) + 2Br^-(aq) \rightarrow Br_2(aq) + 2Fe^{2+}(aq)$

Overall $E^\ominus = 2 \times 0.77 - 1.09 = +0.45\,V$

So the reaction can take place and you will see brown bromine in solution and the yellow Fe^{3+} would go green.

🅔 Student A correctly predicts the outcome of the possible reactions and scores 4 marks. However, the statement that iodine is produced is just a statement and not a description of what would be seen so no marks are scored for that part.

Student B takes the trouble to give the correctly balanced overall equations but this leads to an error in interpreting the electrode potential data. It is incorrect to double the value of the electrode potential. They are used as given and no multiplication should be used to match the balancing numbers in the equation. The first prediction is still correct and the examiner would probably allow 2 marks for this but the second prediction is wrong and the student loses these marks. On the other hand the description of the reaction between $Fe^{3+}(aq)$ and $2I^-(aq)$ is correct, so Student B's overall mark is 3.

Student A

(c) $2I^-(aq) \rightarrow I_2(aq) + 2e^-$ $\times 5$

$5e^- + MnO_4^-(aq) + 8H^+(aq) \rightarrow Mn^{2+} + 4H_2O(l)$ $\times 2$

Overall equation is:

$10e^- + 2MnO_4^-(aq) + 16H^+(aq) + 10I^-(aq) \rightarrow 2Mn^{2+} + 5I_2(aq) + 4H_2O(l) + 10e^-$

Questions & Answers

(c) $2I^-(aq) \rightarrow I_2(aq) + 2e^-$

$5e^- + MnO_4^-(aq) + 8H^+(aq) \rightarrow Mn^{2+} + 4H_2O(l)$

which means:

$2MnO_4^-(aq) + 16H^+(aq) + 10I^-(aq) \rightarrow 2Mn^{2+} + 8H_2O(l) + 5I_2(aq)$

e In this part Student B does better than Student A and gets all 3 marks. Student A gets 1 mark but might be awarded 2 marks. The multiplication factor for each of the two half-equations has been identified correctly but there are two errors in the overall equation.

The $10e^-$ should not be included and, although the examiner might be prepared to accept this, the student has put $4H_2O(l)$ on the right-hand side of the equation instead of $8H_2O(l)$ and this means 1 mark is definitely lost. When combining half-equations it is easy to forget to multiply all the components by the necessary factor. It is always a good idea to have a good look at what you have done to try and avoid the error.

e **Overall, Student A scores 11 or 12 out of 14 marks, while Student B scores 11.**

Question 18 Transition metals

(a) **(i)** What is meant by the term transition element? (2 marks)

(ii) Complete the electron configuration of the iron atom:
$1s^2\,2s^2\,2p^6\,...$ (1 mark)

(iii) Write the electron configuration of Fe^{2+} and Fe^{3+} ions. (2 marks)

(b) **(i)** Aqueous Fe^{2+} ions react with aqueous hydroxide ions.
Write an ionic equation for this reaction and state what you would see. (2 marks)

(ii) The product formed in the reaction between aqueous Fe^{2+} ions and aqueous hydroxide ions slowly darkens and eventually turns 'rusty'.
What has happened to cause this colour change? (1 mark)

(c) The dichromate ion, $Cr_2O_7^{2-}$, is an oxidising agent that can be used in laboratory analysis. It reacts with acidified Fe^{2+} ions to form Cr^{3+} and Fe^{3+} ions:
$Cr_2O_7^{2-}(aq) + 14H^+(aq) + 6e^- \rightarrow 2Cr^{3+}(aq) + 7H_2O(l)$
$Fe^{2+}(aq) \rightarrow Fe^{3+}(aq) + e^-$

(i) Construct the full ionic equation for this reaction. (1 mark)

(ii) Calculate the volume of $0.0100\,mol\,dm^{-3}$ potassium dichromate required to react with $20.0\,cm^3$ of $0.0500\,mol\,dm^{-3}$ acidified iron(II) sulfate. (3 marks)

Total: 12 marks

e The command word 'construct' in part (c)(i) indicates that you must use the information given in the question to obtain the full ionic equation.

> **Student A**
>
> (a) (i) An element that forms one or more stable ions that have partly filled d-orbitals.

> **Student B**
>
> (a) (i) An element that has partly filled d-orbitals.

e Student A gets both marks but Student B scores only 1 mark. There are two key marking points: 'partly filled d-orbitals' is essential but it must also be clearly stated that the element forms one or more ions that have partly filled d-orbitals.

> **Student A**
>
> (a) (ii) $1s^2\ 2s^2\ 2p^6\ 3s^2\ 3p^6\ 3d^6\ 4s^2$

> **Student B**
>
> (a) (ii) $1s^2\ 2s^2\ 2p^6\ 3s^2\ 3p^6\ 4s^2\ 3d^6$

e Both students get the mark. The order of $3d$ and $4s$ is acceptable as either $3d$ followed by $4s$ or vice versa. However, if it is written as $4s^2\ 3d^6$ mistakes might be made when it comes to writing electron configurations of ions.

> **Student A**
>
> (a) (iii) Fe^{2+}: $1s^2\ 2s^2\ 2p^6\ 3s^2\ 3p^6\ 3d^6$
>
> $\qquad\quad Fe^{3+}$: $1s^2\ 2s^2\ 2p^6\ 3s^2\ 3p^6\ 3d^5$

> **Student B**
>
> (a) (iii) Fe^{2+}: $1s^2\ 2s^2\ 2p^6\ 3s^2\ 3p^6\ 4s^2\ 3d^4$
>
> $\qquad\quad Fe^{3+}$: $1s^2\ 2s^2\ 2p^6\ 3s^2\ 3p^6\ 4s^2\ 3d^3$

e Student A gets both marks but Student B fails to score. The way in which Student B wrote the configuration for the Fe atom in (a)(ii) reflects the fact that the $4s$-subshell fills before the $3d$-subshells. However, the danger of writing it this way is that when ions are formed, the tendency is to remove electrons from the $3d$-orbitals first, when in fact the first electrons to be lost are always the outer electrons (in this case, the electrons in the $4s$-orbital).

> **Student A**
>
> (b) (i) $Fe^{2+}(aq) + 2OH^-(aq) \rightarrow Fe(OH)_2(s)$
>
> $\qquad$ Green precipitate

Questions & Answers

Student B

(b) (i) $Fe^{2+} + 2OH^- \rightarrow Fe(OH)_2$

$Fe(OH)_2$ is a blue–green gelatinous precipitate.

e Both get 2 marks.

Student A

(b) (ii) Fe^{3+} is more stable than Fe^{2+} and therefore iron(ii) compounds are readily oxidised. The rust colour is due to $Fe(OH)_3$ being formed.

Student B

(b) (ii) $Fe(OH)_3$ is a rust–brown gelatinous precipitate and therefore $Fe(OH)_2$ must have changed to $Fe(OH)_3$.

e Both students get the mark.

Student A

(c) (i) $Cr_2O_7{}^{2-} + 14H^+ + 6Fe^{2+} \rightarrow 6Fe^{3+} + 2Cr^{3+} + 7H_2O$

Student B

(c) (i) $Cr_2O_7{}^{2-} + 14H^+ + 5e^- + Fe^{2+} \rightarrow Fe^{3+} + 2Cr^{3+} + 7H_2O$

e Student A gets the mark but Student B does not. The full ionic equation does not contain any electrons. It is essential to scale the two half-ionic equations so that the electrons cancel out.

Student A

(c) (ii) mols of $Fe^{2+} = \dfrac{0.0500 \times 20.0}{1000} = 0.001\,mol$

mols of $Cr_2O_7{}^{2-} = 6 \times$ moles of $Fe^{2+} = 0.001 \times 6 = 0.006\,mol$

$1\,dm^3$ contains $0.01\,mol$ of $Cr_2O_7{}^{2-}$

So volume of $Cr_2O_7{}^{2-} = \dfrac{0.006}{0.01} = 0.6 = 600\,cm^3$

Student B

(c) (ii) moles of $Fe^{2+} =$ moles of $Cr_2O_7{}^{2-} = 0.0500 \times \dfrac{20.0}{100} = 0.001\,mol$

$V = \dfrac{n}{c} = \dfrac{0.001}{0.01} = 0.1\,dm^3 = 100\,cm^3$

e Both students get 2 marks out of 3 but for different reasons. Student A has correctly calculated the moles of Fe^{2+} but has multiplied this value by 6 instead of dividing it by 6. Student B has calculated the moles of Fe^{2+} correctly, but he/she has not used the 1:6 molar ratio. Titrations calculations are usually designed so that the volume added from the burette is around $25\,cm^3$. Calculations rarely involve volumes over $50\,cm^3$. The answers obtained by both students should have prompted them to check their calculations for errors. The correct value is $16.7\,cm^3$.

e Overall, Student A scores 11 out of 12 and Student B scores 7.

Extended-response questions

Question 19 Transition metals and stereoisomerism

(a) Explain the meaning of the terms 'ligand' and 'coordinate bond'.　　　　(2 marks)

(b) Stereoisomerism is sometimes shown by transition metal complex ions. Using a suitable named example in each case, show how transition metal complex ions can form:

　　(i) *cis–trans* isomers

　　(ii) optical isomers　　　　(8 marks)

(c) Ligand exchange can often occur when transition metal complex ions react. These exchanges will take place if a new complex ion can be formed that has a greater stability. An example of a ligand exchange reaction is the formation of $[CoCl_4]^{2-}$ from $[Co(H_2O)_6]^{2-}$.

　　Describe how you would convert $[Co(H_2O)_6]^{2+}$ into $[CoCl_4]^{2-}$ and what you would see as the reaction took place.　　　　(3 marks)

Total: 13 marks

e Part (b) is a free-response question and requires careful planning. There are 8 marks available so it is likely that eight different points have to be made. The question is divided into parts (i) and (ii) so it is likely that 4 marks will be allocated to each part. Each type of isomerism is best illustrated using suitably labelled diagrams.

Student A

(a) A ligand is a lone pair donor. A coordinate bond is the same as a dative bond.

Student B

(a) A ligand is a lone pair donor. A coordinate bond is formed between the ligand and the vacant *d*-orbitals of the Fe^{2+}. The ligand supplies both electrons for the bond.

---

e Student A scores only 1 mark as the definition of a coordinate bond is insufficient. Student B gets both marks as detail is provided in the explanation of coordinate bond.

Student A

(b) (i) *Cis–trans* isomerism occurs when a complex has two different ligands. In one version the ligands of one type are alongside each other while in the other version they are opposite. An example is the dichloro-diamminonickel complex shown below.

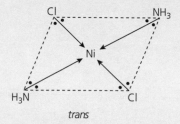
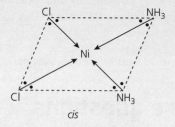

trans   *cis*

(ii) Optical isomerism occurs when one stereoisomer is a reflection of the other. The ligands must be bidentate. An example is with nickel. The ligand is shown as a double-headed arrow in my diagram.

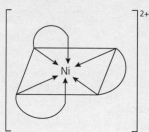
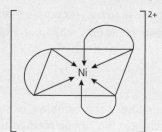

As you can see the second version is a reflection of the first and it is non-superimposable.

Student B

(b) (i) Nickel can form a complex ion containing ammonia and chloride. In the one version of the complex the ammonia molecules are next to each other and so are the chloride ions. This is called *cis*. But also they might be opposite each other across the complex ion and then it would be *trans*.

(ii) Optical isomers occur when you have ligands that attach at two points on the metal ion. Nickel forms one of these as well. If you have three of them they can be attached and then there are two versions that are mirror images of each other.

e The marking points for this question are:

- *cis–trans*: named example ✓, give shape ✓, explanation of difference between *cis–trans* ✓, identify *cis* and *trans* correctly ✓

- optical: named example ✓, explain multidentate ligand required ✓, explain isomers are reflections of each other ✓, indicates how the ligands are attached ✓

Student A has done well and has made a good attempt to explain the two types of isomerism. The use of clear diagrams earns almost all the marks. For *cis–trans* all the marks could be obtained from a clearly labelled diagram and for optical isomerism all but 1 mark is possible. Student A gets 7 of the 8 marks in this way but an actual example of a complex ion showing optical isomerism is not given, which loses 1 mark.

Student B may know the answer but tries to answer the question without using diagrams. This is almost impossible. Perhaps the third and fourth marks can be awarded for the *cis–trans* explanation and the second and third for the optical isomerism, giving a total of 4 marks.

Student A

(c) The addition of chloride ions will convert $[Co(H_2O)_6]^{2+}$ into $[CoCl_4]^{2-}$. You would see the pink solution of $[Co(H_2O)_6]^{2+}$ change to a blue colour, showing that $[CoCl_4]^{2-}$ had been made.

Student B

(c) Excess concentrated hydrochloric acid must be added to the water complex ion. When it is added the colour change that occurs is from pink to blue.

---

e Student B obtains all 3 marks, but Student A earns only 2 marks because he/she leaves out the excess chloride ions.

e **Student A has done well, scoring 10 out of 13 marks. Student B obtains 9 marks.**

Question 20 Qualitative analysis

The labels have fallen off of six bottles of chemicals. The labels were: manganese(ii) chloride, iron(ii) chloride, copper(ii) sulfate, manganese(ii) nitrate, ammonium(ii) sulfate and chromium(iii) nitrate.

Devise a series of tests that would enable you to distinguish which is which.

You must state the reagents that you would use and the observations that you would expect to make. Write equations for any reactions that occur.

Total: 22 marks

e This question will require a very structured response. There are a variety of ways of tackling the question and the mark scheme will be flexible to allow for different approaches. It is important to include what has been requested in the question, so reagents and observations must be included, together with equations for each reaction.

Questions & Answers

Test for a chloride   Add $AgNO_3$ solution separately to a solution of each of the unknowns. The two that give white precipitates are the two chlorides $MnCl_2$ and $FeCl_2$:

$$Cl^-(aq) + Ag^+(aq) \rightarrow AgCl(s)$$

Solutions of $MnCl_2$ and $FeCl_2$ can then be reacted with $NaOH(aq)$ and the Mn will give a reddish/brown precipitate and the Fe will give a greenish precipitate.

Test for a sulfate   Add $BaCl_2(aq)$ to the other four solutions and the Cu and ammonium will both give precipitates:

$$SO_4^-(aq) + Ba^{2+}(aq) \rightarrow BaSO_4(s)$$

Add $NaOH(aq)$ separately to $CuSO_4$ and the $(NH_4)_2SO_4$ — $CuSO_4(aq)$ gives a blue precipitate and the ammonium compound doesn't give a precipitate:

$$Cu^{2+}(aq) + 2OH^-(aq) \rightarrow Cu(OH)_2(s)$$

The remaining two solutions must be the nitrates: $Cr(NO_3)_3$ and $Mn(NO_3)_2$. Add $NaOH(aq)$ to each and the Cr will give a green precipitate and Mn a reddish/brown precipitate:

$$Cr^{3+}(aq) + 3OH^-(aq) \rightarrow Cr(OH)_3(s)$$

$$Mn^{2+}(aq) + 2OH^-(aq) \rightarrow Mn(OH)_2(s)$$

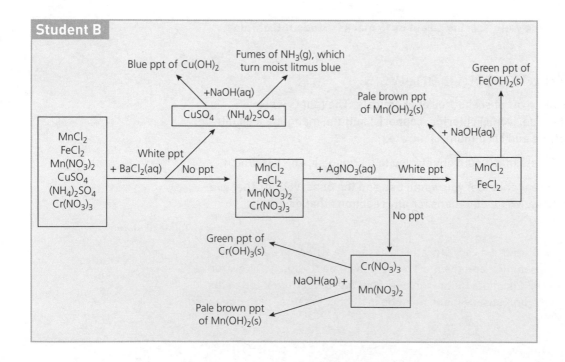

e Both the students have made good attempts at answering this question. They have approached it in very different ways. In awarding the marks, deductions have been for errors and omissions. Both students have elected to identify the anions first but it is equally valid to start with the metal cations.

Student A has been reasonably systematic and scores well. Unfortunately they started by testing for the chloride, which is a mistake as the sulfates would also have precipitated because Ag_2SO_4 is insoluble. This would lose 2 marks. The only other error is that when NaOH is added to an ammonium salt, $NH_3(g)$ is evolved, which would turn litmus red. They have systematically written all the equations and cleverly written the tests for the cations as ionic equations. Student A would score 18 or 19 out of 22.

Student B's approach is very different and very good. The flow diagram shows clearly all the reagents and the observations — they are carried out in the correct sequence and the chemistry is faultless. However, Student B has not written any equations for any of the reactions that occur. This is very costly as there is a total of eight equations, so unfortunately Student B loses 8 marks and scores 14 out of 22.

The responses to this question emphasise how important it is to *read* the question carefully. Both students' answers are good and Student A, despite making mistakes, gets a grade-A score. Student B makes no mistakes but forgets to include the equations, and this means that only a grade-C score is achieved.

Question 21 Synoptic question

Copper reacts with nitric acid, HNO_3, but the products of the reaction depend upon the concentration of the acid.

If the acid is dilute then the following reaction takes place:

copper + dilute nitric acid

$Cu(s) \rightarrow Cu^{2+}(aq) + 2e^-$

$4H^+(aq) + NO_3^-(aq) + 3e^- \rightarrow NO(g) + 2H_2O(l)$

If the nitric acid is concentrated then the reaction is:

copper + concentrated nitric acid

$Cu(s) \rightarrow Cu^{2+}(aq) + 2e^-$

$2H^+(aq) + NO_3^-(aq) + e^- \rightarrow NO_2(g) + H_2O(l)$

(a) Write balanced equations for each of the above reactions. (5 marks)

(b) In an experiment, some nitric acid is reacted with 1.27 g of copper and it is found that 320 cm^3 of gas is produced. Deduce whether the acid used in this experiment was dilute or concentrated.

   Show *all* your working. (4 marks)

Total: 9 marks

Questions & Answers

ℯ Part (a) is fairly straightforward — you have to use the half-equations provided to determine the overall ionic equations. Part (b) is much more difficult; you have to relate the moles of Cu and the moles of gas to your full ionic equations. The command words in this question are deliberately vague.

Student A

(a) The electrons have to balance, hence for dilute acid:

$Cu(s) \rightarrow Cu^{2+}(aq) + 2e^-$; multiply by 3

$4H^+(aq) + NO_3^-(aq) + 3e^- \rightarrow NO(g) + 2H_2O(l)$; multiply by 2

$3Cu(s) \rightarrow 3Cu^{2+}(aq) + 6e^-$

$8H^+(aq) + 2NO_3^-(aq) + 6e^- \rightarrow 2NO(g) + 4H_2O(l)$

Balanced equation is:

$8H^+(aq) + 2NO_3^-(aq) + 3Cu(s) \rightarrow 3Cu^{2+}(aq) + 2NO(g) + 4H_2O(l)$

For concentrated acid:

$Cu(s) \rightarrow Cu^{2+}(aq) + 2e^-$

$2H^+(aq) + NO_3^-(aq) + 1e^- \rightarrow NO_2(g) + H_2O(l)$; multiply by 2

$Cu(s) \rightarrow Cu^{2+}(aq) + 2e^-$

$4H^+(aq) + 2NO_3^-(aq) + 2e^- \rightarrow NO_2(g) + H_2O(l)$

Balanced equation is:

$4H^+(aq) + 2NO_3^-(aq) + Cu(s) \rightarrow Cu^{2+}(aq) + NO_2(g) + H_2O(l)$

Student B

(a) Dilute nitric:

$8H^+(aq) + 2NO_3^-(aq) + 3Cu(s) \rightarrow 3Cu^{2+}(aq) + 2NO(g) + 4H_2O(l)$

Conc. nitric:

$4H^+(aq) + 2NO_3^-(aq) + Cu(s) \rightarrow Cu^{2+}(aq) + 2NO_2(g) + 2H_2O(l)$

ℯ The marking points for this question are:

- dilute acid — multiply copper half-equation by 3 ✓, multiply acid half-equation by 2 ✓, correct balanced equation ✓
- concentrated acid — multiply acid half-equation by 2 ✓, correct balanced equation ✓

Student A gets all 3 marks for the equations for the dilute acid but carelessly loses 2 marks for the concentrated acid equations by failing to multiply the product side of the equation by 2.

Student B poses a dilemma for the examiner. Clearly, he/she is able and has correctly deduced the balanced equations for both reactions, but not all of the working has been shown. Student B would probably get 4 of the 5 marks.

Student A

(b) With dilute nitric acid, 3 mol of Cu will produce 2 mol of NO(g).

With concentrated nitric acid, 1 mol of Cu will produce 1 mol of NO_2(g).

The amount in moles of copper reacted is $\dfrac{1.27}{63.5} = 0.02$.

The amount in moles of gas produced is $\dfrac{320}{24000} = 0.0133$.

Mole ratio Cu:gas

0.02:0.0133

1.5:1

∴ 3:2

3 mol of Cu produce 2 mol of gas and therefore the acid must be dilute.

Student B

(b) moles of Cu used = 0.02

moles of gas = $\dfrac{320}{24} = 13.3$

e The marking points for this question are: moles of copper used ✓, moles of gas produced ✓, molar ratio Cu:gas ✓, relate molar ratio to correct equation ✓.

Student A scores the final 4 marks by deducing correctly that the dilute acid was used.

Student B scores 1 mark for the moles of copper used but scores no more marks. In the final part of the calculation Student B has incorrectly divided $320\,cm^3$ by $24\,dm^3$ and this has given a value that does not relate to either equation and Student B is, therefore, unable to continue with the calculation.

e **Overall, Student A scores 7 out of 9 marks even though one of the equations is wrong. Student B, who correctly gives both equations, only scores 5 out of 9 marks.**

Knowledge check answers

1 a rate would double

b rate would decrease by factor of 4 (quartered) $(\frac{1}{2})^2 = \frac{1}{4}$

c rate would increase by factor of $3 \times 3^2 = 27$ times faster

2 a units of k are $dm^6\,mol^{-2}\,s^{-1}$ or $mol^{-2}\,dm^6\,s^{-1}$

b units of k are $dm^{12}\,mol^{-4}\,s^{-1}$ or $mol^{-4}\,dm^{12}\,s^{-1}$

3 Using experiments 1 and 2: concentration of $[BrO_3^-]$ is doubled and the rate doubles. Therefore the reaction is first order with respect to $[BrO_3^-]$.

Using experiments 2 and 3: concentration of $[Br^-]$ is doubled and the rate doubles. Therefore the reaction is first order with respect to $[Br^-]$.

The units of the rate constant show that the overall reaction is fourth order. Therefore the reaction is second order with respect to $[H^+]$.

4 slow step $ICl + H_2 \rightarrow HCl + HI$

fast step $HI + ICl \rightarrow HCl + I_2$

The two steps add up to give the overall equation: $2ICl + H_2 \rightarrow 2HCl + I_2$

5 A **reversible reaction** is a reaction that proceeds in both the forward and the reverse reactions.

A **dynamic equilibrium** is when the rate of the forward reaction equals the rate of the reverse reaction so that the reagents and products are constantly interchanging (**dynamic**) but the concentrations are constant (**equilibrium**).

le Chatelier's principle states that a closed system under equilibrium will adjust to any external changes by moving in such a way as to minimise the effect of the external change.

6 Low temperature would favour the forward exothermic reaction, so the equilibrium would move to the right-hand side.

High pressure would move the equilibrium position to the right because there are fewer moles of gas on the right-hand side.

7 a $K_c = [NO_2]^2/[N_2O_4]$

b i equilibrium moves to the right; therefore it turns darker brown

ii equilibrium moves to the left; therefore it turns paler brown

iii no effect — stays the same

8 a units = $dm^3\,mol^{-1}$ (or $mol^{-1}\,dm^3$)

b units = $dm^3\,mol^{-1}$ (or $mol^{-1}\,dm^3$)

9 Number of moles of each gas must be divided by the volume $(4\,dm^3)$ in order to get the concentrations of each gas:

$[N_2] = 1.25$, $[H_2] = 2.5$, $[NH_3] = 1.25$

$K_c = 1.25^2/(1.25 \times 2.5^3) = 0.08\,dm^6\,mol^{-2}$

10 There is an equal number of moles of gas on each side of the equation. Therefore K_c does not have any units and it does not matter whether you use the number of moles or the concentration of each component — the answer will be the same.

number of moles of each gas at equilibrium: $H_2(g)$ = 0.3, $I_2(g)$ = 0.2, $HI(g)$ = 0.2

concentration of each gas at equilibrium: $[H_2(g)]$ = 0.15, $[I_2(g)]$ = 0.1, $[HI(g)]$ = 0.1

using moles: $K_c = 0.2^2/(0.3 \times 0.2) = 0.67$

using concentrations: $K_c = 0.1^2/(0.15 \times 0.1) = 0.67$

11 a mole fraction of gas A = $\dfrac{0.1}{0.1 + 0.4 + 0.6} = \dfrac{0.1}{1.1} = 0.091$

mole fraction of gas B = $\dfrac{0.4}{0.1 + 0.4 + 0.6} = \dfrac{0.4}{1.1} = 0.364$

mole fraction of gas C = $\dfrac{0.6}{0.1 + 0.4 + 0.6} = \dfrac{0.6}{1.1} = 0.545$

b partial pressure of gas A = $0.091 \times 200 = 18.2$ kPa

partial pressure of gas B = $0.364 \times 200 = 72.8$ kPa

partial pressure of gas C = $0.545 \times 200 = 109$ kPa

12 a units = kPa^{-1}

b units = kPa^{-1}

13

	$PCl_5(g)$	$\rightleftharpoons$ $PCl_3(g)$	+ $Cl_2(g)$
Initial moles	0.15	0	0
Equilibrium moles	0.05	0.1	0.1
Mole fractions	0.2	0.4	0.4
Partial pressures	22	44	44

$K_p = \dfrac{44 \times 44}{22} = 88\,kPa$

14 a $CH_3COO^-K^+$

b $(HCOO^-)_2Mg^{2+}$

c $Ca^{2+}{}_3(PO_4{}^{3-})_2$ (could also form $Ca^{2+}HPO_4{}^{2-}$ or $Ca^{2+}(H_2PO_4{}^-)_2$)

15 a OH^-

b $SO_4{}^{2-}$

c $NH_2{}^-$

d $C_6H_5COO^-$

16 a H_3O^+

b H_2SO_4

c $NH_4{}^+$

d $CH_3NH_3{}^+$

17 $CH_3CO_2H + HNO_3 \rightleftharpoons CH_3CO_2H_2{}^+ + NO_3{}^-$

18 a **i** 2   **ii** 1.3   **iii** 5.82

b **i** 3.55×10^{-7} **ii** 5.62×10^{-4} **iii** 5.62×10^{-2}

19 a pH = 1.0

b pH = 2.0

c pH = 3.0

20 B, A, C

21 $6.3 \times 10^{-5}/(1.7 \times 10^{-5}) = 3.7$ times stronger

22 As temperature increases so does K_w, therefore so does $[H^+(aq)]$ and $[OH^-(aq)]$, hence increasing temperature moves the equilibrium to the right indicating that the forward reaction is endothermic and ΔH will therefore be positive.

23 a pH = 0.82

  b pH = 5.07

  c pH = 13.18

  d moles of unreacted HCl = 0.01 in $30\,cm^3$ solution
  concentration of unreacted HCl = $0.333\,mol\,dm^3$
  pH of solution = 0.48

24 If HIn represents the formula of bromocresol green, then $K_{In} = [H^+][In^-]/[HIn]$. $[In^-]$ is blue and [HIn] is yellow. The green colour will be formed when $[In^-]$ = [HIn] such that $K_{In} = [H^+]$. The pH when the green colour is formed is 4.7.

25 a $\frac{1}{2}Cl_2(g) \rightarrow Cl(g)$

  b $Ca^{2+}(g) + 2Cl^-(g) \rightarrow CaCl_2(s)$

  c $Mg^+(g) \rightarrow Mg^{2+}(g) + 1e^-$

26 a $MgBr_2$, NaBr, KBr

  b CaF_2, $CaCl_2$, $BaCl_2$, $BaBr_2$

27 a $Ca^{2+}(g) + aq \rightarrow Ca^{2+}(aq)$

  b $Ca(OH)_2(s) + aq \rightarrow Ca^{2+}(aq) + 2OH^-(aq)$

  c $Ca^{2+}(g) + 2OH^-(g) \rightarrow Ca(OH)_2(s)$

28 a ΔS will be negative (the movement of particles in ice is more restricted)

  b ΔS will be positive (the particles in an aqueous solution have more freedom to move than particles in the solid)

  c ΔS will be negative (the oxygen molecules have reacted and are not free to move)

  d ΔS will be negative (the reduction in overall volume as the reaction takes place reduces the freedom to move)

29 The equation for the reaction is $2Na(s) + \frac{1}{2}O_2(g) \rightarrow Na_2O(s)$
  The entropy change, ΔS, is $72.8 - ((2 \times 51.0) + (\frac{1}{2} \times 102.5)) = -80.5\,J\,mol^{-1}\,K^{-1}$

30 a $MnO_4^-(aq) + 8H^+(aq) + 5V^{2+}(aq) \rightarrow 5V^{3+}(aq) + Mn^{2+}(aq) + 4H_2O(l)$

  b $3MnO_4^-(aq) + 24H^+(aq) + 5V^{2+}(aq) + 15H_2O(l) \rightarrow 5VO_3^-(aq) + 30H^+(aq) + 3Mn^{2+}(aq) + 12H_2O(l)$
  This is simplified by cancelling the H^+ and H_2O that appear on both sides of the equation to give:
  $3MnO_4^-(aq) + 5V^{2+}(aq) + 3H_2O(l) \rightarrow 5VO_3^-(aq) + 6H^+(aq) + 3Mn^{2+}(aq)$

  c $Cr_2O_7^{2-}(aq) + 14H^+(aq) + 3SO_2(aq) + 6H_2O(l) \rightarrow 3SO_4^{2-}(aq) + 12H^+(aq) + 2Cr^{3+}(aq) + 7H_2O(l)$
  This can then be simplified to:
  $Cr_2O_7^{2-}(aq) + 2H^+(aq) + 3SO_2(aq) \rightarrow 3SO_4^{2-}(aq) + 2Cr^{3+}(aq) + H_2O(l)$

  d $8H^+(aq) + 2NO_3^-(aq) + 3Cu(s) \rightarrow 3Cu^{2+}(aq) + 2NO(g) + 4H_2O(l)$

31 a $Mg(s) \rightarrow Mg^{2+}(aq) + 2e^-$ $E^{\ominus} = +2.37\,V$
  $Zn^{2+}(aq) + 2e^- \rightarrow Zn(s)$ $E^{\ominus} = -0.76\,V$
  Therefore the overall cell potential is 1.61 V.

  b $Fe^{3+}(aq) + e^- \rightarrow Fe^{2+}(aq)$ $E^{\ominus} = +0.77\,V$
  $Sn^{2+}(aq) \rightarrow Sn^{4+}(aq) + 2e^-$ $E^{\ominus} = -0.15\,V$
  Therefore the overall cell potential is 0.62 V.

  c $Br_2(aq) + 2e^- \rightarrow 2Br^-(aq)$ $E^{\ominus} = +1.09\,V$
  $2I^-(aq) \rightarrow I_2(aq) + 2e^-$ $E^{\ominus} = -0.54\,V$
  Therefore the overall cell potential is 0.55 V.

  d $Zn(s) \rightarrow Zn^{2+}(aq) + 2e^-$ $E^{\ominus} = +0.76\,V$
  $I_2(aq) + 2e^- \rightarrow 2I^-(aq)$ $E^{\ominus} = +0.54\,V$
  Therefore the overall cell potential is 1.30 V.

  e $Br_2(aq) + 2e^- \rightarrow 2Br^-(aq)$ $E^{\ominus} = +1.09\,V$
  $Sn^{2+}(aq) \rightarrow Sn^{4+}(aq) + 2e^-$ $E^{\ominus} = -0.15\,V$
  Therefore the overall cell potential is 0.94 V.

32 a 1.25 V

  b $2NiO(OH) + 2H_2O + Cd \rightleftharpoons 2Ni(OH)_2 + Cd(OH)_2$

  c The battery can be recharged by applying an external voltage that reverses the reactions above.

33 Overall reaction: $C_2H_5OH + 3O_2 \rightarrow 2CO_2 + 3H_2O$
  Reaction at the oxygen electrode: $3O_2 + 12H^+ + 12e^- \rightarrow 6H_2O$
  Reaction at the ethanol electrode: $C_2H_5OH + 3H_2O \rightarrow 2CO_2 + 12H^+ + 12e^-$
  The two reactions at the electrodes cancel and simplify to give the overall reaction.

34 a +2 **b** +2 **c** +3 **d** +2 **e** +3

35 a 6 **b** 2 **c** 6 **d** 6

36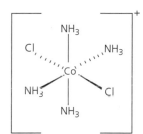

Shape is octahedral, bond angles are 90°, the oxidation number of the Co is +3 and the type of isomerism is *cis–trans*

en = $H_2NCH_2CH_2NH_2$

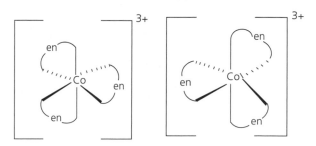

Shape is octahedral, bond angles are 90°, the oxidation number of the Co is +3 and the type of isomerism is optical isomerism

37 a $4NH_3 + [Cu(H_2O)_6]^{2+} \rightarrow [Cu(NH_3)_4(H_2O)_2]^{2+} + 4H_2O$

   b $Cl^- + [Co(NH_3)_6]^{3+} \rightarrow [Co(NH_3)_5Cl]^{2+} + NH_3$

   c $SCN^- + [Fe(H_2O)_6]^{3+} \rightarrow [Fe(H_2O)_5(SCN)]^{2+} + H_2O$

38 moles of $S_2O_3^{2-}$(aq) = 1.80×10^{-3} = moles of Cu^{2+}

   mass of Cu^{2+} = $1.80 \times 10^{-3} \times 63.5 = 0.1143\,g$

   %Cu = $(0.1143/0.426) \times 100 = 26.8\%$ (to 3 s.f.)

39 In this question there may be other tests that are valid.

   a Add aqueous silver nitrate to a solution of each of the compounds. The chloride would form a white precipitate of silver chloride.

   b Add aqueous barium nitrate to a solution of each of the compounds. The sulfate will form a white precipitate of barium sulfate.

   c Add excess aqueous sodium hydroxide to a solution of each of the compounds. Each will initially form a precipitate of a hydroxide. $Cu(OH)_2$ would be blue and $Cr(OH)_3$ would be green. But the chromium hydroxide will dissolve in excess aqueous sodium hydroxide.

   d Add aqueous sodium hydroxide to a solution of the compounds. Each forms a precipitate of a hydroxide, but iron(II) hydroxide is green and iron(III) hydroxide is rust/brown.

   e Add aqueous sodium hydroxide to a solution of each of the compounds. Each forms a precipitate of a hydroxide but iron(II) hydroxide is green and manganese hydroxide is pale pink/white. (Both would gradually turn brown.)

Note: **bold** page numbers indicate defined terms.

Index